DAVENANT RETRIEVALS seek to exemplify the Davenant Institute's mission of recovering the riches of the Reformation for the contemporary church, offering clear, concise, and collaborative expositions of a doctrinal topic key to the Protestant heritage and defending its relevance today.

PEOPLE OF THE PROMISE:
A MERE PROTESTANT ECCLESIOLOGY

Edited by Joseph Minich
and Bradford Littlejohn

Front cover image taken from Marion Post Wolcott, *Baptism in Triplett Creek, KY* (1940; G. Gibson Gallery, Seattle, WA)

Cover design by Rachel Rosales, Orange Peal Design

LIST OF CONTRIBUTORS

Joseph Minich is a graduate of Reformed Theological Seminary in Washington D.C. and is currently pursuing a Ph.D in Humanities at The University of Texas at Dallas. Some of his writing can be found at *The Calvinist International* and *Mere Orthodoxy*.

Bradley Belschner is a systems analyst at EMSI, an economic modeling firm, a determined generalist, and an enthusiast of Reformation theology. He has served as a co-editor of the Modernization of Richard Hooker's *Lawes* project.

Steven Wedgeworth (M.Div., Reformed Theological Seminary) is the pastor of Christ Church of Lakeland, Florida (CREC). Steven has published essays on politics, theology, and history, and is the co-founder and editor of *The Calvinist International*.

Alastair Roberts (Ph.D, University of Durham) is a leading evangelical blogger and author of several forthcoming books, including *Heirs Together: A Theology of the Sexes* and *Echoes of Exodus: Tracing Themes of Redemption through Scripture* (both Crossway, forthcoming 2018). He blogs at www.alastairadversaria.com and also serves as Editor of the Politics of Scripture section of *Political Theology Today*.

E.J. Hutchinson (Ph.D, Bryn Mawr College) is Associate Professor of Classics at Hillsdale College (Hillsdale, Mich.), where he has taught since 2007. His research interests focus on the literature of Late Antiquity and the

Neo-Latin literature of the Renaissance and Reformation, and he is translating Niels Hemmingsen's *De Lege Naturae* for the Sources in Early Modern Economics, Ethics, and Law series. He is a member of the Orthodox Presbyterian Church.

Bradford Littlejohn (Ph.D, University of Edinburgh) is the President of the Davenant Institute and teaches philosophy at Moody Bible Institute (Spokane). He is the author of four books, most recently *The Peril and Promise of Christian Liberty: Richard Hooker, the Puritans, and Protestant Political Theology* (Eerdmans, 2017), and has published numerous articles and book chapters in historical theology and Christian ethics. He also serves as an Associate Editor of *Political Theology*.

Andre Gazal (Ph.D, Trinity International University) teaches at Trinity Evangelical Divinity School, the University of Northwestern Ohio, and North Greenville University. He is the author of *Scripture and Royal Supremacy in Tudor England: The Use of Old Testament Historical Narrative*. He has also contributed to the *Encyclopedia of Christianity in the United States* (Rowman and Littlefield, 2016) and the *Encyclopedia of Martin Luther and Reformation* (Rowman and Littlefield, forthcoming 2017).

Jordan Ballor (Dr. theol., University of Zurich; Ph.D, Calvin Theological Seminary) is a senior research fellow at the Acton Institute for the Study of Religion & Liberty in Grand Rapids, Mich. He is the author of *Get Your Hands Dirty* (Wipf and Stock, 2013), *Covenant, Causality, and Law* (Vandenhoeck and Ruprecht, 2012, and editor of many other volumes).

Jake Meador is the Vice President of the Davenant Institute and Editor-in-Chief of Mere Orthodoxy. He lives in Lincoln, NE with his wife and two children. He is the author of *Searching for Shelter: The Quest for Community in a Fractured and Furious World* (IVP, forthcoming 2018). His writing has appeared in *First Things*, *Books & Culture*, *Front Porch Republic*, *Christianity Today*, and *Fare Forward*.

Andrew Fulford is a Ph.D candidate at McGill University, where he is researching the relationship of Richard Hooker's thought to narratives of the emergence of secularity in the early modern period. He is the author of *Jesus and Pacifism: An Exegetical and Historical Investigation* (Davenant, 2016), and essays on John Calvin and Richard Hooker.

For Peter Escalante
Mentor and Friend

CONTENTS

Part IV: Protestant Ecclesiology Today

PREFACE

Bradford Littlejohn

THE TASK of the present volume is, at first glance, a simple one: to present the basic core of the Protestant doctrine of the church, shorn of the distractions of the secondary disputes about polity, ministerial offices, sacramental efficacy, liturgy and more that have so often preoccupied discussions of the church. Of course, precisely because such disputes have often elevated these second-order issues to first importance, this task is not so simple. Certainly, it cannot claim to be a mere descriptive task, as if we were pretending to function merely as historians, investigating the history and founding documents of the Protestant churches to find the shared kernel concealed in the variegated husks of the Reformation traditions. No, our endeavor here is in large part a normative one, and unabashedly so. We aim to present in clear outline form what the basic principles of Protestant ecclesiology *should* look like, as an offering to a church today bewildered by the myriad of fashionable models on offer.

Of course, ours is not, we hope, an arbitrary ecclesiological wish list vying for attention amidst these fashionable models. In other words, although it is not merely descriptive, neither is it merely normative. On the contrary, it is built on the fruits of three descriptive tasks (as all good Protestant theology should be): an exegetical description of the revealed content of the Scriptures, an historical description of the central claims of the Reformation and post-Reformation dogmatics, and a dogmatic description of what, according to the internal logic of Protestantism's claims, must be its true doctrine of the church. These three tasks correspond loosely to the Parts II through IV of the book, respectively, though to some extent, each is operative in greater and lesser degree at every point.

The kind of exegetically and dogmatically guided historical retrieval, in service of an urgent contemporary need, and thus presented in accessible prose without needless footnoting frills, is what we seek to model in the new series of which this book is the first offering, Davenant Retrievals. Readers familiar with our recent publication efforts may recognize some similarity to the objective of our Davenant Guides, which "seek to offer short and accessible introductions to key issues of current debate in theology and ethics, drawing on a magisterial Protestant perspective and defending its contemporary relevance today." The difference is our Davenant Guides are intended to be very short, introducing a single neglected key concept or commitment within magisterial Protestantism (though one that may be very broad in its implications), whereas Davenant Retrievals aim to present a multi-faceted view of an entire dogmatic locus, drawing on the expertise of a range of contributors. Each volume in this series, we envision, will be the result of a series of essays appearing in the themed quarterly issues of our journal, *Ad Fontes*, subsequently expanded and revised, together with perhaps a couple of new contributions. Most of the essays in this volume, accordingly, appeared in their original form in the September 2016, December 2016, March 2017, and June 2017 issues of *Ad Fontes*, under the indefatigable supervision of my dear friend Joseph Minich and the longsuffering layout expertise of Rachel Rosales. The essays for next year's volume of Davenant Retrievals, beginning to appear now in *Ad Fontes*, are slated to address the role of philosophy within theology.

As with any multi-contributor volume, the immense gain that comes from sharing the insights and gifts of many writers certainly comes with drawbacks. Although the various contributors are remarkably like-minded when it comes to the principal arguments of this volume, there are certainly differences at least of emphasis amongst us, and we have not tried to smooth these out into an entirely homogeneous whole. The end result, we believe, is consistent and coherent—indeed, rather more so than we had dared hope when we embarked on the project—but reflects some of the creative tensions and paradoxes that are part and parcel of Protestant theology. Readers may perhaps be frustrated by the topics and questions that receive little or no coverage in this volume; part of this is inevitable in any short introduction, but part is also a difficult-to-avoid feature of the multi-contributor format. These represent *essays toward* a systematic exposition of a Protestant ecclesiology, illuminating the subject from many different partial yet complementary angles, but we would certainly not claim that the volume itself contains such a full systematic exposition.

Such apologies once made, it remains to offer a brief outline of the organizational shape of the volume in the form it now appears. The basic logic of the volume is clear enough from the four main headings in the Table of Contents. Part I, Introduction to Protestant Ecclesiology, seeks to situate the main claims of the Protestant doctrine of the church in both contemporary and historical context. The first task is undertaken by Joseph Minich's essay, "The Church Question in a Disoriented Age," which seeks to understand why it is that Protestants today find ourselves so desperate to make sense of the doctrine of the church and to restore it to some place of centrality, though often a misplaced centrality. The second task is accomplished in Bradley Belschner's pithy and pungent, "The Protestant Doctrine of the Church and its Rivals," which aims to cut through the fog of history and get to the nub of the matter: there are, and have been, only a handful of internally-consistent options for ecclesiology, and magisterial Protestantism is, not to put too fine a point on it, the best of them.

Part II, Protestant Ecclesiology in Scripture, aims to fortify this claim via what, for Protestants at least, is the strongest evidence of all, the testimony of Scripture. Although certainly not attempting a full or systematic survey of all the biblical teaching on the doctrine of the church, these essays illuminate the basic contours through a consideration of the church in the Old Testament (Steven Wedgeworth), the etymology of the word *ekklesia* (E.J. Hutchinson), and the foundations of the New Testament church in the Book of Acts (Alastair Roberts). Collectively, these essays help sustain our basic thesis: that the church is, quite simply, the people of the promise, the gathered assembly of all those who call on the name of the Lord, with institutional trappings playing a supportive rather than constitutive role.

Part III, Protestant Ecclesiology in History, extends and nuances this picture via a consideration of how the dynamic of the church's invisibility and visibility, and its visibility *qua* organic and *qua* institutional, to use Abraham Kuyper's language, played out in the Reformation and the formulations that emerged from it. Once again, and perhaps even more emphatically so, the essays seek merely to pick out key themes and moments, though my own essay, "*Simul Justus et Peccator*: The Genius and Tensions of Protestant Ecclesiology," is intended to serve as at least something of an "Idiot's Guide to Reformation-era Ecclesiologies." Dr. Andre Gazal complements this narrative with a close reading of how the understanding of ordained ministry was transformed in the early Church of England from a sacerdotal to an evangelical and proclamatory office. In describing the Church of England as emphatically united with the Continental Protestant ecclesiological consensus, both these essays certainly challenge generations of Anglican self-understanding, but not in a way that would raise many eyebrows among professional historians nowadays. Dr. Jordan Ballor's excursus on church discipline singles out a key theme of Reformed Protestantism in particular and offers a Biblical and pastoral defense and clarification of its role in the church.

This sets the stage for Part IV, Protestant Ecclesiology Today. This begins by finally undertaking a more systematic dogmatic statement of Protestant ecclesiology, in the form of Andrew Fulford's essay "Protestant Ecclesiology as Good Theory." Fulford's essay, however, is more than merely a dogmatic statement; it also endeavors to drive home the thesis—an underlying thesis of the whole book—that Protestant ecclesiology simply makes sense of the world, our experience, and the central claims of the Christian faith in a way much more plausible and simple than alternative ecclesiologies. Finally, Jake Meador seeks to spell out some of the practical import of the doctrine in his essay, "Protestant Ecclesiology Among Contemporary Political Theologies." In it, he makes the provocative case that magisterial Protestant ecclesiology holds the best answer to contemporary confusion over the role of Christianity in public life, and of how Christians should and should not endorse liberal political order.

Joseph Minich concludes by reminding us that the unity and holiness of the church must always be an already and a not yet, and that "to wish for a less messy ecclesiology is perhaps to unwittingly rob God of His honor." Surrounded as we are today by cries for the church to get its act together and overcome the scandal of its divisions, it is important for us to take a step back and resist the idolatry that can creep into such cries. We have no business being complacent about the church's imperfections, but we have no business being alarmist either; they are a salutary reminder that the church we see is not the church that God sees, or the church that he is, amidst all our sinful stumblings, building up out of living stones.

PART I:
AN INTRODUCTION TO PROTESTANT ECCLESIOLOGY

I.

THE CHURCH QUESTION IN A DISORIENTED AGE

Joseph Minich

NO QUESTION is approached from nowhere. It always begins with questioners. Who are the *we* asking the question of ecclesiology? What concerns make up our world? And, likewise, to what sorts of problems do we imagine the question of ecclesiology to provide a potential solution?

In this particular case, we the questioners are inhabitants of late modernity and its concerns. Chief among these is the liquid nature of modern identity—wherein "all that is solid melts into air."[1] Most humans in history have navigated their way through this world suspended atop given identities—including identities of time, place, culture, language, religion, nuclear and extended family, local customs, gender, etc. The late modern world, by contrast, while one of comparative technological comfort, is an age of anxiety as it pertains to our sense of the self and our relationship to a larger community. The causes are manifold and need

---

[1] The origin of this phrase is Karl Marx's *The Communist Manifesto* (1848). It was later appropriated by Marshall Berman in his *All That is Solid Melts Into Air: The Experience of Modernity* (New York: Penguin, 1982).

not detain us here. But not a few commentators have iden-tified the modern West (and particularly America) as deep-ly fractured, a place and a time wherein basic identities cannot be taken for granted.[2] This is the case whether we speak of individuals, groups, or the whole of society. Like a man staring at a mirror in a dark room, we are easily dis-oriented in relation to the larger space around us—and the identities which have historically helped us navigate this space now reflect back its confusion rather than its illumi-nation.

It is in this situation that *we* ask questions about the church. Consequently, we tend to approach the question concerning ecclesiology as a question related to authority, identity, and community. It is worthy to note, in this re-gard, how the same concerns show up in apparently differ-ent conversations. The debate over what it means to be "Reformed," for instance, largely parallels the debate over what it means to be American, the relationship between American values and documents, the debate over what America's "trajectory" and "story" are, etc. And, indeed, there are not even settled and commonly agreed upon ref-erence points. All of us are necessarily left to exercise judgment in piecing these things together. It is not clear whether we are receiving and passing on the original or its distortion, especially since our intellectual exemplars are never without equal among those who inflect our heritage differently than we do. We are left, therefore, with two options. We can either outsource our judgment or we can exercise a significant degree of agency in seeking to be per-

---

[2] See, for instance, Zygmund Bauman, *Liquid Modernity* (New York: Polity, 2000), and Daniel Rodgers, *Age of Fracture* (Cambridge: Harvard University Press, 2011).

suaded concerning wisdom. In either case, we all find ourselves addressing these questions via an intellectual collage—an attempt to piece together a picture of reality from a massive pile of particulars, an ambiguous sense of the end product, and (what is key) the felt arbitrariness of our particular community's vision of reality alongside our freedom to abandon it.

OUR CONCERNS: THE "WHAT" OF OUR CHURCH QUESTION

This is our situation, and in it, our world of concern and our sought-for reference points will tend to revolve around questions of reliable authority and stable community. Given the massive confusion in which we find ourselves, who has the right to define what it means to be American, to be Reformed, to be a Christian? Who has the right to define the implicit content of these terms? And what are the essential truths or essential markers that unite persons in a group and in a project despite their differences? These questions are obviously related. To ask what unites a group of persons is, in our world of freedom and disagreement, also to ask who has the authority to make a judgment call concerning this question. Ironically, however, the problem of skepticism and its inevitable termination in submission to a person or to a community who reasons on your behalf, is a hallmark of *modern* rather than ancient thought. Not the act of outsourcing itself, of course, but rather the contention that such outsourcing is *inevitable* for the finite person. While it is popular to locate the origin of Modern skepticism in Renaissance finitude or in Reformation individualism-cum-Enlightenment, its practical "on the ground" hold was arguably birthed in the Roman counter-

Reformation and its attempt to render the Reformation vulnerable on precisely the question of epistemic chaos.[3]

In any case, *our* question concerning ecclesiology is a question of community and of authority. Movements as diverse as Reformed confessionalism, the recent version of "two kingdoms" theology, the Federal Vision, the New Perspectives on Paul, Radical Orthodoxy, neo-Anabaptism, The Emerging Church movement, the Acts 29 movement, the shepherding movement among charismatics, the popularity of 9Marks ministries among Baptists—all have the doctrine of the church at their forefront. Each is interested in how the church is the "family and house of God" and how we can know its content and members. Their emphases differ in terms of high and low ecclesiologies, in their relative emphasis on the church as an organism or as an institution, on the church as visible or as invisible, as local institution or as a family of the baptized across geographic or political boundaries, on the church as a people or as a place, as the new humanity and solution to human strife or as the antithesis to the world, as a voluntary society or as a unique polis with its own distinctive government, weapons, and charter, etc. But all are united in addressing *our* questions of community and of authority in thinking about the doctrine of the church.

OUR SOLUTIONS: A FEW CONTEMPORARY RESPONSES TO THE CHURCH QUESTION

There is, of course, nothing innately problematic about this state of affairs. We cannot escape ourselves or our

---

[3] See Richard Popkin, *The History of Skepticism: From Savonarola to Bayle* (New York: Oxford University Press, 2003).

questions. But our questions conceal as much as they reveal, limiting (as they do) the potential resonances between ourselves and the reality with which we are attempting to come to terms. For instance, a renewed emphasis on the church's authority, on its spiritual power, on reading the Bible with the church, on the democracy of the dead, on the recovery of church fathers, sacramental life, corporate liturgy, and even on the church as the site of our "eternal family" and "eternal identity" vis and vis our temporal identities and families—are frequently employed in ways that create more problems than they solve.

Let us take, for instance, the notion of the church's "spiritual" power or "spiritual" authority.[4] It is normally emphasized, at least in Reformed circles, that this does not refer to something beyond the authority of the Word itself. But then the question becomes what the difference is between the authority of the institutional church and the authority of an individual Christian with respect to the object of judgment. If a church falsely condemns someone (say, Martin Luther), then there are no spiritual implications. Conversely, if a church fails to condemn someone (say, Pope Alexander VI), the spiritual "power" of judgment obtains no matter what the church says or does. Nor, in each of these cases, is the church's pronouncement or lack of it binding on the conscience of any believer. What happens when the church makes such pronouncements? Certainly there might be earthly communal and political implications, but ultimate spiritual implications are neither cre-

---

[4] I am thinking here in particular of Jonathan Leeman, *The Church and the Surprising Offense of God's Love: Reintroducing the Doctrines of Church Membership and Discipline* (Wheaton: Crossway, 2009), and David Van Drunen, *Living in God's Two Kingdoms: A Biblical Vision for Christianity and Culture* (Wheaton: Crossway, 2010).

ated nor prevented in the church's pronouncements. Its spiritual power is simply the power that the Word has by itself. And the Word, in simple point of fact, can be channeled by both the church as an institution and by an individual believer. Who, for instance, would deny that many have been converted because an ordinary layperson shared God's Word of promise with another person?

Similarly, let us take the language of the "church as polis," or the church as our "eschatological family"[5]—our identity in which shall outlast our identity as members of our natural families. Well, everything depends upon what this means, and it has often meant something quite classically cultish. For instance, while our corporate identity in Christ will obtain in eternity, the particular "local church" of which we are a part will not. This local institutional expression of the church is actually temporal in all of its particulars. The eternal bond we have with one another is a bond we also have with all other believers—including those in our family and, in principle and potential, with all persons. The relationship between our temporal and eternal identities, then, does not map neatly onto institutional boundaries. And when they are forced to, pastoral dangers await. Many churches, for instance, insist on the local church as one's primary site of obligation and focus, over against one's obligation to their natural family or even to other institutional churches. Inevitably, this confusion of categories leads to the attempted binding of a free conscience.

As a final example, let us consider what is meant by the recent popularity of the phrase "Reformed catholici-

---

[5] See Jonathan Leeman, *Political Church: The Local Assembly as Embassy of Christ's Rule* (Downers Grove: InterVarsity Press, 2016).

ty."[6] Normally contrasted to more "narrow" Reformed (or "True Reformed") ethos, Reformed "catholicity" is concerned about the church fathers, about sacraments, about liturgy, etc. It often remains ambiguous, however, whether the Reformed tradition itself contains essential deficiencies in this area. Does the Reformed tradition require principled supplementation from other groups so that we can arrive at some hoped for *tertium quid*—a new age for the church? Or is "catholicity" a call for Reformed persons to take up what is already part of their heritage at its best and in principle? Often, it means the former, and the inevitable "supplementations" rather quickly strike at what are arguably "essentials" of Reformed identity while preserving those bits which are "accidental" only.[7] The continuity implied in the "Reformed" part of "Reformed Catholic" is, then, superficial.

REFORMING THE QUESTIONS

In all of the above examples, lack of clarity inevitably terminates in pastoral and theological malpractice. Often, lack of clarity reveals that formulations have been developed in reaction to other errors rather than in conversation with reality as such. Discourse concerning church authority, for instance, is often a reaction to the perceived problem of individualism and autonomy rampant in America. What is

---

[6] Most popularly in Michael Allen and Scott Swain, *Reformed Catholicity: The Promise of Retrieval for Theology and Biblical Interpretation* (Grand Rapids: Baker Academic, 2015).

[7] I made this point at slightly more length in "And What is Reformed Calvinism," *The Calvinist International*, April 22, 2015, https://calvinistinternational.com/2015/04/22/and-what-is-reformed-catholicism/.

at stake in discussing the church as a "polis" is often the idolatrous marriage of the gospel of Christ with the agencies of empire. Reformed Catholicism, as I have mentioned, postures itself over against an aggressively ignorantly but nevertheless confident and navel-gazing community which cannot imagine the larger world of ecclesiastical discourse—and often of its very own history!

And yet, while each of these might be considered legitimate concerns, theological and pastoral formulations shaped around them will only tend to be their alter-ego. It is not, of course, that these problems and the questions they pose cannot be a spring-board into the reality at stake in the doctrine of the church. But it is precisely *reality*, fine-grained observation, and first principles which must be sought if we are to develop adequate theological and pastoral tools to navigate our modern situation in all of its difficulty. And it is the judgment of this book that the early Protestant claim concerning the church's definition and essence really did capture precise *reality* as it pertains to the "what" of the church. It becomes our calling, then, to appropriate their insight as we ask the question concerning ecclesiology in our context. While there is much positive theological work to build on top of this, the guiding principle in all Protestant ecclesiology faithful to its founding insight is simply this: *The church, at its most basic, is just the people of the promise.* This is all that is absolutely *necessary* for there to be "the church." Other things might be normative, but this is the "essential form"—the most basic thing. The church is the community of those who have been claimed by God's promise—who have said "yes" to the gospel message.

But surely, one might think, this is trivial. What is at stake in this claim? This book attempts to present this basic Reformation insight to a modern audience. Of first importance is that the *church does not make the Word, but that the Word makes the church*. The conscience of the Christian, therefore, is bound only in relation to God speaking through His Word and His world. The church's authority might be declaratory or persuasive, but it never stands in any absolute sense "between" the believer and the Word. Furthermore, the church is where the gospel is believed. While it is normative (and indeed, in a very distinctive sense, necessary) to be marked out by baptism and the Lord's Supper, these do not have the same type of *absolute* necessity as the promise itself. The believer in prison, in fellowship with other believers in prison (even if forced *not* to receive baptism) is no less a member of the visible church than the apostle Paul. And note this third emphasis, then. Even what we call the *visible* church is prior to any of its institutional expressions. The church is more like an extended family with many institutional expressions, but it is most fundamentally the fellowship of those who are marked out by gospel profession. While the church is normatively (but not essentially) made objective in baptism, this normative/essential distinction is crucial for discussing the "essence" of the church. And, let it be admitted, we are not left without ambiguity. Like any Italian family, there are in-fights about which members are the purest Italians, and fights about who is not Italian at all. There are arguments about whose food (or doctrine) is the best, whose practices are the least authentic, who has deviated the furthest from Romulus and Remus, etc.

Be that as it may, the ambiguity is not one of our making, but rather maps precisely onto reality as it has always been actually experienced in the Christian church. The modern condition only makes this more clear. Even if a Medieval Christian, for instance, thought they were a member of the church because they were in communion with the bishop of Rome, their subjective belief about what makes them a member of the church does not change the fact that *we* can claim them even if they wouldn't claim us. Why? Because we do not define the family the same way they do. We claim them as family because we claim as family anyone who believes God's gospel promise. Children of the Reformation can claim Augustine and Anselm and Aquinas as our forefathers just as much as a Roman Catholic can. The Reformation did not create a different church. It was and is a purifying movement within the *one* church, the *one* family of God, which cannot (even in its visibility) be conflated with any single earthly institution.

REFORMING THE QUESTIONERS

It is urgent that we grasp how radical this Reformation claim was. A Christian living in those tumultuous times might have perceived much continuity of liturgy, church structure, and even of doctrine—but the entire definition of what the church was had changed. Its essential relation to the Word had changed. The relation of the latter to the individual and his or her conscience changed. And, bringing us full circle, these sorts of emphases might be alarming to those who are reacting to modernity. Even if the Reformation clarified our principles and re-defined the essence of the church, did it not also lead to all of *our* problems? Was it not through the world created by the Reformers that we have received a culture rife with church division, individualism, idolatrous nationalism, etc.?[8]

Of course, as one might suspect, "it's complicated." More urgent, however, than expounding this answer is getting at the anxiety itself. Can the Protestant doctrine of the Christian conscience, of its freedom in relation to God's Word, and of the priesthood of all believers in their common relation to the gospel be abused? Absolutely. But they are also simply reality. Even Rome has had to concede that it cannot technically force someone to go against their conscience and that the church has (at times) erred in failing to condemn one or failing to receive another. But it is just this—a concession. And even Rome technically admits that the unbaptized person on the island can be in Christ. But this is an afterthought to the definition of the church. The Reformers integrated these two concessions into the very definition of the church and its authority. And the resulting focus concerned essentials—the hard lines of reality—the fruit of which is a tremendous theological cash-value in the actual world, as actually lived.

Take, for instance, our anxiety concerning individualism. Arguably, the Reformation doctrine (Luther's two kingdoms of Christ's immediate reign in the soul versus the mediation of human governments in church, state, and family) captures precisely what remains both "individual" and "corporate" in the lived world and in Scripture. Paul, for instance, tells the Galatians that they are free in Christ, but that they must not use their freedom as an opportunity

---

[8] As seems to be the charge of, for instance, Brad Gregory, *The Unintended Reformation: How a Religious Revolution Secularized Society* (Cambridge: Harvard University Press, 2012).

to serve the flesh. Note that this abuse is not a condemnation of freedom. The freedom is rather for obedience and maturity. And so with the doctrine of the Reformers. The doctrine of the free conscience in relation to the Word can certainly be abused by cocky persons who pretend that they do not need anyone. It can certainly be abused as a recipe for laziness and sloth. But the Reformation never intended to fully avoid these things because these things *cannot* be fully avoided. Rather, the freedom of the conscience, and the building of ecclesiastical and civil institutions around an honoring of this basic insight, is a call to both individuals and to communities *to grow up*! Individuals are called to submit to earthly authorities within their legitimate jurisdictions (Luther's "three orders" of ecclesial, civil, and familial) and earthly governments are called to recognize the pretension of attempting to manipulate a free conscience that they cannot and should not ultimately attempt to control. As it pertains to matters of conscience, then, the resultant trajectory is the development of a culture of persuasion.

In any case, maturation requires a significant degree of individuality—ownership over one's convictions, personal persuasion, a seeking to stand on one's own two feet confidently in Christ. Note, then, that Paul expected the Galatians to be aware if even he himself taught a different gospel! He expected them to be confident in the face of angels and apostles who taught something other than the gospel of Christ. This expectation necessarily assumes confident and persuaded believers—mature conviction. But the expectation of maturity leaves room for the possibility of abuse and of failure. This is precisely why Paul warns against it. Our calling to read the Bible with the church, then, is transformed in this light. It is not that the church fathers have a special "spiritual authority" that our Christian neighbor does not. Rather, *not* to read the Bible with those who spent their lives reading and bleeding for it is, in a word, stupid. It would likewise be immature for a physicist to neglect the works and insights of other physicists and the corporate judgments of the physics community. In this context, catholicity is more an ethos than a supplement to a perceived problem of insularity. A devolution from basic principles already bedevils the latter—principles which would rather demand a wise self-awareness such that confidence was had in proportion to one's actual competence. The irony is that the flame of catholic doctrine burns hottest when it is preserved through channels of persuasion. We carry the torch because we believe the promise and its doctrinal explication as it has been proclaimed to us. As agents who have freely received and imbibed the proclamation, we are then driven to pass it on to other agents by the very same means of persuasion.

CONCLUSION: A CALL TO MATURITY

Finally, then, this call to maturity can be either killed or cultivated by a culture's choices concerning the legitimate uses of persuasion and coercion. The world that grew out of the Reformation was a world which increasingly demanded persons to come to convictions about their faith—to own it through their own agency. And this is admittedly a scary prospect. The most prominent live options seem to be insecurity and hubris. But a culture whose main goal is to avoid either will, to that extent, avoid wisdom as well. Fortunately, what stands behind this call to maturity is precisely what we need to attain it. To wit, the free Christian knows local churches and nations to constitute "penultimate" identities. We are united to Christ through His Word and to one another through love, and this is our ultimate identity. The shakiness and confusion of our earthly identities (whether ecclesiastical, civil, familial, etc.), while perhaps a matter of great importance, are suspended atop something absolutely and eternally solid. And this encourages the very mental and spiritual relaxation that helps us to cultivate wisdom, to love finitude, and to pursue the truth *together*. In this light, there need be no anxiety or skepticism to parasitically feed off of one another. The most basic things—that we are children of the most high God (made in His image), forgiven through the death and resurrection of Jesus Christ, and called to maturity through His Spirit—do not render all other things dispensable, but rather dependent on deeper fundamentals. And these fundamentals become an anchor to the questioner in the storm of his or her questions—reference points of reality for a pilgrim people who still cling to a promise. In my judgment, these reference points have never been more insightfully captured than in Luther's famous words in his 1520 *On the Freedom of a Christian*: "A Christian is a perfectly free lord of all, subject to none. A Christian is a perfectly dutiful servant of all, subject to all." One way of summarizing the project before us is to say that it is an attempt to understand this one statement more fully—and in so doing to demonstrate that ecclesiology, rather than a weakness of Protestantism, is one of its greatest strengths. Such is our attempt to honor and cultivate that flame that started five hundred years ago.

THE PROTESTANT DOCTRINE OF THE CHURCH AND ITS RIVALS

Bradley Belschner

DESPITE the multitude of ecclesiologies practiced and defended throughout Christian history, they can all be boiled down to four consistent options:

- Papal sacerdotalism (Roman Catholicism)
- Magisterial sacerdotalism (e.g., Eastern Ortho-doxy)
- Magisterial evangelicalism (e.g., historic Protestants)
- Anarchic evangelicalism (e.g., Anabaptists like the Amish and Mennonites)

The most important distinction above is sacerdotal vs. evangelical. Sacerdotalism refers to the role of the "priest" as a spiritual mediator between God and man, and also the notion that bishops represent the apostles by virtue of apostolic succession. In this view the clergy do not exist merely to promote good order in the church; rather, their offices are imbued with unique spiritual power that lay Christians do not possess. The church is conceived of as an institution, and the boundary of that institution is defined by the clergy. Roman Catholics and Eastern Orthodox affirm different versions of sacerdotalism, since the former insists on a supreme Roman bishop within the clergy, but either way both churches share the same fundamental belief in the mediatorial role of the clergy.[1]

Evangelicalism, on the other hand, affirms the universal priesthood of all believers. Christ is the only true mediator between God and man, and consequently we should not believe our church leaders are imbued with any magical power by virtue of their status; rather, their role is to promote good order in the human society that we call the visible church community. Evangelicals believe that wherever two or three believers are gathered, there you will find the church. This core belief is shared by both Magisterial Protestants and Anabaptist Protestants. (For the purposes of this essay "protestant" and "evangelical" are used synonymously.)

The second distinction is Papal vs. Magisterial vs. Anarchic. This distinction concerns the relationship of the church to temporal society, especially civil government.

Papal ecclesiology, strictly speaking, teaches that *all civil and spiritual power* on earth is invested in the Roman Pontiff. Dogmatically the Pope has been given authority

---

[1] Many historic Protestants have maintained some attenuated version of this theory, unwilling to let go of the idea that a special spiritual power is conferred at ordination. If by this they mean something over and beyond the spiritual importance of temporal order and leadership in the church, and distinct from the recognition that the Spirit uniquely equips ministers to carry out their appointed tasks (as indeed He equips all Christians to carry out their callings), we must demur. This would be a remnant of sacerdotalism and an inconsistency within Protestant ecclesiology; cf. Bavinck's *Reformed Dogmatics* (Grand Rapids: Baker House Company, 2008), 1:381-83.

over all kings and civil magistrates. By divine right the two swords of spiritual and civil power both belong to the Pope, and he merely delegates the usage of one sword to the civil magistrate. Crazy as this may sound to us today, the doctrine is actually enshrined in *Unam Sanctam*, the papal bull issued by Boniface VIII in 1302 AD:

> Certainly the one who denies that the temporal sword is in the power of Peter has not listened well to the word of the Lord commanding: 'Put up thy sword into thy scabbard' [Mt 26:52]. Both, therefore, are in the power of the Church, that is to say, the spiritual and the material sword, but the former is to be administered for the Church but the latter by the Church; the former in the hands of the priest; the latter by the hands of kings and soldiers, but at the will and sufferance of the priest. However, one sword ought to be subordinated to the other and temporal authority subjected to spiritual power.[2]

Consequently, the Pope has authority to coerce the faith. In Rome, spiritual authority has temporal teeth. It is no accident that Roman Catholics historically set up systematic inquisitions and burned heretics; the Pope is explicitly and theologically granted the authority to perform

---

[2] "Unam Sanctam: One God, One Faith, One Spiritual Authority," *Papal Encyclicals Online*, accessed on August 15, 2016, http://www.papalencyclicals.net/Bon08/B8unam.htm.

such coercion, though of course he may also exercise gentler measures as he sees fit.[3]

But let's not forget about that first sword in *Unam Sanctam*, the spiritual one. He owns that one too. As Boniface says,

> We believe in [the Church] firmly and we confess with simplicity that outside of her there is neither salvation nor the remission of sins. [...] we declare, we proclaim, we define that it is absolutely necessary for salvation that every human creature be subject to the Roman Pontiff.

In other words, the Pope is a *sine qua non* for salvation. It's not hard to find statements like this in Roman Catholicism. They are not anomalies. In 1516 the Fifth Lateran Council—to Catholics the infallible 18th ecumenical council—reasserted the authority of *Unam Sanctam* and reiterated its claims:

> since subjection to the Roman pontiff is necessary for salvation for all Christ's faithful, as we are taught by the testimony of both sacred scripture and the holy fathers, and as is declared by the constitution of pope Boniface VIII of happy memory, also our predecessor, which begins Unam sanctam, we therefore, with the approval of the present sacred council, for the salvation of the souls of the same faithful, for the supreme authority of the Ro-

---

[3] For an excellent treatment of this by a Roman Catholic philosopher, see Professor Thomas Pink's paper, "What is the Catholic doctrine of religious liberty?" available online at several locations, but available at https://www.academia.edu/639061/What_is_the_Catholic_doctrine_of_religious_liberty (accessed September 8, 2016).

man pontiff and of this holy see, and for the
unity and power of the church, his spouse, re-
new and give our approval to that constitution.[4]

Inevitably, therefore, the Roman Catholic version of
sacerdotalism overlaps with their doctrine of temporal
government: in both cases the Pope reigns as the supreme
figure on earth.

Magisterialism denies this vehemently. For magisteri-
als of both sacerdotal and evangelical persuasion—both
Eastern Orthodox and historic Protestants—the *civil magistrate* is the guardian of the church. The Second Helvetic
Confession describes his role as such:

> THE MAGISTRACY IS FROM GOD. Mag-
> istracy of every kind is instituted by God him-
> self for the peace and tranquillity of the hu-
> man race, and thus it should have the chief
> place in the world. If the magistrate is op-
> posed to the Church, he can hinder and dis-
> turb it very much; but if he is a friend and
> even a member of the Church, he is a most
> useful and excellent member of it, who is able
> to benefit it greatly, and to assist it best of all.

> THE DUTY OF THE MAGISTRATE. The
> chief duty of the magistrate is to secure and
> preserve peace and public tranquillity. Doubt-
> less he will never do this more successfully
> than when he is truly God-fearing and reli-
> gious; that is to say, when, according to the

---

[4] Note also that they call the church the "spouse" of the
Roman pontiff! See "Fifth Lateran Council," *Legion of Mary
- Tidewater, Virginia*, accessed on August 15, 2016,
http://www.legionofmarytidewater.com/faith/ECUM18.HTM.

example of the most holy kings and princes of the people of the Lord, he promotes the preaching of the truth and sincere faith, roots out lies and all superstition, together with all impiety and idolatry, and defends the Church of God. We certainly teach that the care of religion belongs especially to the holy magistrate.[5]

The Westminster Confession of Faith (1646) elaborates and provides a more detailed job description:

The civil magistrate may not assume to himself the administration of the Word and sacraments, or the power of the keys of the kingdom of heaven: yet he hath authority, and it is his duty, to take order, that unity and peace be preserved in the Church, that the truth of God be kept pure and entire; that all blasphemies and heresies be suppressed; all corruptions and abuses in worship and discipline prevented or reformed; and all the ordinances of God duly settled, administered, and observed. For the better effecting whereof, he hath power to call synods, to be present at them, and to provide that whatsoever is transacted in them be according to the mind of God.[6]

---

[5] *Second Helvetic Confession,* chapter XXX, *Christian Classics Ethereal Library,* accessed August 15, 2016, https://www.ccel.org/creeds/helvetic.htm.

[6] *Westminster Confession of Faith,* chapter XXIII, *Center for Reformed Theology and Apologetics,* accessed August 15, 2016, http://www.reformed.org/documents/westminster_conf_of_faith.html . The 1788 American revision of the Westminster Confession wisely modifies this section, instead describing a much more hands-off role for the civil magistrate in ecclesiastical affairs.

This is not a uniquely Protestant position. An historically minded Eastern Orthodox Christian would cheerfully agree here. However, there are tensions in Eastern Orthodoxy between their sacerdotalism and magisterialism—what is their institutional church, a holy thing or a civil temporal thing? In Magisterial Protestantism the principles are much clearer. For us the visible church is, by definition, a temporal human society. And of course, the civil magistrate is the man charged with promoting peace and order within temporal human society.

As the old trope goes, all laws legislate morality; the only question is which morality. In other words, all government promotes a particular vision of the common good, of religion, of justice. This is how we answer questions like: *What is marriage? Do prayers belong in school? Should scientologists receive 501c3 tax exempt status?* etc. Like it or not, our government currently makes decisions regarding all these questions. Magisterial Protestantism simply teaches that they should form such judgments in a Christian manner. For example, we could argue that a member of ISIS should be deported from the USA *because of his religion*. Not all false religions are created equal. Some are fine to passively tolerate, like a grumpy atheism. Other religious sects pose dangerous threats to the peace and common good, and on that basis the civil magistrate should weed them out.

It may sound strange to speak about the civil magistrate in such explicitly Christian terms, but frankly, what is the alternative? An officially agnostic and functionally atheist secular government? Perhaps no civil government at all? That last option is basically the anabaptist position. Anabaptists like the Amish and Mennonites are anarchists, strictly speaking, insofar as they believe civil government should be eliminated entirely and the peaceful church should reign in its place. They believe promoting justice and peace via the sword, coercively, is counterproductive and contrary to Jesus' commands. Consequently, the anabaptists are pacifists and refrain from most participation in government.

Putting this all together then, we get the four main ecclesiologies listed above.[7] In theory each group is clean and theologically distinct, but in practice it gets a lot messier. Not all individuals are aware of their group's guiding principles, and those who are aware do not necessarily stay faithful to them.

Roman Catholics today have tried to backpedal away from the sort of extreme statements made in their 18th ecumenical council. But of course they aren't allowed to backpedal, because their dogma is infallible, so they're stuck between a rock and a hard place. The result was the second Vatican council in the 1960s, the hard place crushing them. This famously ambiguous synod introduced an ecclesiological fog that still enshrouds Roman Catholicism. Regardless of such doctrinal obfuscations, it must be granted that Popes today certainly act a lot less papal than in previous centuries. There's no risk of Pope Francis I burning anybody at the stake, or damning Christians who don't have faith in him. So although the Pope technically

---

[7] Technically we might add a fifth ecclesiology, *anarchic sacerdotalism*. If any church matches this description it would be Coptic Orthodoxy. They've been living under disapproving civil magistrates for 15 centuries, ever since they rejected the Imperially-approved Council of Chalcedon in 451. Historically their church has been somewhat associated with pacifism and extreme monastics. However, their overall ecclesiology is ambiguous, and it would be unfair to straightforwardly characterize them as 'anarchic' in the same way that modern Mennonites are.

has not renounced any of these ecclesiological errors, he at least has the good character to live in denial that the worst of these errors ever existed.

Eastern Orthodoxy has historically been magisterial, and in some places like Russia this emphasis is on the rise again. However the Eastern Orthodox church in America is much less magisterial, and in some quarters is leaning towards pacifism and a vaguely anabaptist view of government[8], though usually not in a consistent or wholesale way.

Both the Roman Catholic and Eastern Orthodox churches are just as sacerdotal as ever, though in America this is downplayed a bit and they also emphasize personal Bible reading and other stereotypically evangelical practices.

Traditional Protestants in America—Baptists, Presbyterians, Lutherans, Anglicans, Methodists, etc.—are today largely unaware of their historical tradition and its corresponding philosophical and biblical exegesis, particularly as it relates to the civil magistrate, and consequently they tend to default to a semi-anabaptist ecclesiology. Even tenets of outright anabaptism are becoming easier to find, with advocates for pacifism and political withdrawal growing louder each year. Overall in our Western and increasingly post-Christian society, anabaptist flavors of ecclesiology seem to be strengthening in every Christian group. Nevertheless, on the whole American Protestants retain vaguely magisterial instincts, as seen in petitions to publicly display

---

[8] E.g., F. Alexander Weber, *The Moral Argument Against War in Eastern Orthodox Theology* (San Francisco: International Scholars Publications, 1998).

the Ten Commandments at courthouses, a desire for our political candidates to be overtly Christian, etc.

WHERE DID THESE ECCLESIOLOGIES COME FROM? A BRIEF HISTORICAL SKETCH

Tracing the historical development of each of these four ecclesiologies is a complex task, but the following sketch should help to orient us historically.

Apostolic Church (1st Century)

The Eucharist was initially coterminous with the agape feast. Practical order necessitated that one man should act as formal leader during the Eucharistic celebration, i.e., somebody had to say the prayer of thanksgiving (the literal meaning of "eucharist"), break the bread, and generally oversee the meal. To quote Walter Lowrie,

> The Eucharistic feast requires a president—that was one of the first suggestions which prompted the development of formal office in the Church. All could not preside at the Eucharist at once, neither was it appropriate that each should preside in turn, from the greatest to the least. Who then shall preside at the Eucharist? The answer presented no theoretical difficulty … substantially it was equivalent to the question, Who, among those present at the particular time and place, is most worthy to sit in the seat of Christ? … it is obvious that in the same community and under the same conditions there would be a certain permanence in the presidency—it was ever the most highly revered disciple that must

> preside. But this did not imply as of necessity
> a formal appointment.[9]

If an apostle was visiting, then obviously he would preside over the Eucharistic feast. Otherwise, the local prophet or charismatic leader would do so. The *Didache*, written in the 1st century, retains this emphasis on the charismatic prophet as the default president for the Eucharist. But what to do if no prophet was available? Enter the bishop or "overseer," the virtuous prophet-substitute. A bishop in the apostolic church was an elder chosen to preside over the Eucharistic feast.

Historically there has been some confusion over the terms "elder" and "bishop", with some arguing they were simply synonyms, but this is only partially true. To quote Lowrie again,

> The name elder indicated originally no formal
> office whatever, but only a vaguely defined
> class of persons who were distinguished for
> their greater age, or longer experience of the
> Christian life. The bishops were selected from
> this class, and so might be spoken of generi-
> cally as elders.[10]

The terms *presbyteros* and *episkopos* in the ancient church should therefore be considered *partial* synonyms, similar to the words "college" and "university" in Ameri-

---

[9] This quote is from page 271 of Walter Lowrie's fantastic book, which we commend to you heartily: *The Church & Its Organization in Primitive & Catholic Times: An Interpretation of Rudolph Sohm's Kirchenrecht* (Longmans: New York, 1904). Available online at https://archive.org/details/churchandorganiz00lowruoft (accessed June 29, 2017).

[10] Lowrie, 276.

can English. The former is a looser and more generic term, whereas the latter is a more specific and formal term. E.g., "I met my wife at college" vs. "Did the candidate attend a university or a community college?"[11]

Of course, none of these guiding offices and roles compromise the doctrine of the priesthood of all believers. Theoretically any believer might be capable of breaking the bread of the Eucharist, but under normal circumstances it made sense and promoted good order and virtue for "elders" in communities to do the "overseeing."

The doctrine of magisterialism was certainly present in the apostolic era, but it might be more accurate to describe it as a theological undercurrent, mostly irrelevant until later centuries. Nevertheless, Paul presumably preached the gospel to the emperor (Acts 9:15, 27:24), and the apostles explicitly commanded Christians to pray for the emperor and to respect his role of promoting peace and order in society (Rom. 13; 1 Tim. 2:1-4; 1 Peter 2:13, 17).

Early Church, Pre-Magistrates (2nd-3rd centuries)

Eventually, as the church grew, Christians separated the Eucharist from the agape feast and combined it with the general service of instruction and worship.[12] This change facilitated larger congregations and greatly increased the formal importance of the bishop's role in presiding over Eucharistic celebration. Over time the office of bishop expanded into the "monepiscopacy" we are familiar with

---

[11] Thanks to Alistair Stewart for this analogy, from *The Original Bishops* (Grand Rapids: Baker Academic, 2014), 13.

[12] Lowrie, 278.

today, with one bishop taking administrative responsibility over multiple congregations. The term "bishop" in this era therefore takes on a new hierarchical meaning, closer to modern usage. Historical evidence indicates that the shift from episcopacy to monepiscopacy emerged in the early 2nd century in some locations, and by the end of the 2nd century it had become pervasive.[13] This administrative evolution seems to have been uncontroversial at the time.

Arguably there is a universal human temptation to sacralize our leaders and treat them as if their office gives them spiritual power, or brings them closer to God somehow. Christians in the early church were no exception, and they fell prey to this temptation. Historical circumstances of persecution probably amplified this tendency. If the church was an army of peace, then the bishops were her generals. Over time it became easy to think of these "generals" as *sine qua nons* of the church, even defining its very structure.

During this era a rudimentary form of sacerdotalism began to sprout, with the clergy mediating as 'priests'. However, it is difficult to tell exactly how 'sacerdotal' these early Christians really were, and how deeply or consistently they followed these tendencies. Some fathers still clearly assumed a universal priesthood over against sacerdotalism,[14] whereas other fathers give us statements that affirm

---

[13] Lowrie, 280.

[14] For example, Tertullian writes, "Are not even we laymen priests? It is written, 'A kingdom also, and priests to His God and Father, hath He made us.' It is the authority of the church, and the honour which hath acquired sanctity through the joint session of the order, which has established the difference between the order and the laity. Accordingly, where there is no joint session of the ecclesiastical order, you offer, and baptize, and are priest, alone for yourself. When three are present, there is the church, although they be laymen" (*De Exhortatione Castitatis*, chap-

sacerdotalism. Many of these sacerdotal statements are ambiguous though and can be interpreted in softer or more pragmatic ways. We must avoid the temptation to anachronistically read current debates back into their texts. It is true that the 20 canons of the council of Nicaea take for granted that the church is structured episcopally, but back then there simply *were* no Christians outside of episcopal structures. It was a simpler and less polarized time, at least in terms of structural ecclesiology.

Magisterialism remained a theological undercurrent. However, we also see a rise in pacifism during this era (which perhaps should not be surprising given the intense persecution). Such pacifist principles were far from universal though. Civil servants who converted to Christianity were generally not expected to leave their posts, unless their office required them to sin or engage in idolatry in some way.[15]

Early Church, Post-Magistrates (4th-5th centuries)

In the 4th century, rulers like Tiridates of Armenia and Constantine of Rome started converting to Christianity, and magisterialism finally came to the forefront. Constantine's conversion is often treated as a watershed moment

---

ter VII in *Fathers of the Third Century: Tertullian, Part Fourth; Minucius Felix; Commodian; Origen, Parts First and Second*, vol. 4 of *The Ante-Nicene Church Fathers* [Buffalo, NY: Christian Literature Publishing, 1885]). Note that Tertullian is not arguing for the priesthood of all believers here. Instead, he is taking it for granted and using it as an uncontroversial premise in order to argue for a different conclusion, namely, the moral superiority of monogamy over bigamy.

[15] For further reading on the complexity of pacifism in the early church, see Phillip Wynn's *Augustine on War and Military Service* (Minneapolis: Fortress Press, 2013).

in Christianity, and rightly so. But the change was primarily a sociological one, not theological. Anabaptists can look back at the church before Constantine and emphasize their favorite elements, like pacifism or hostility between the church and the empire. But after Constantine that narrative can no longer be taken seriously. There can be no pretext of a pacifist, quietistic Christianity after it becomes the official state religion. Christians had been praying for the conversion of the emperor since at least the time of Paul, but it never happened until Constantine.

Magisterialism began to produce good fruit quickly. When the bishops in Constantine's empire could not agree on the divinity of Christ, they appealed to their emperor to help them sort out the issue and enforce the result. It was only natural to invoke his aid in defending the institutional church within his country. In 325 Constantine famously convened the Council of Nicaea.[16] Of course, only the bishops within the borders of the Roman Empire were invited to the council, and the result was only enforced within those borders. It was Constantine who made this ecumenical council possible, and it was only "ecumenical" insofar as he happened to rule over most of the known civilized world at the time.[17] The same applied to the other ecumenical councils in later decades, all of them called by Christian emperors.

---

[16] Roman Catholics claim the Bishop of Rome called the council, but this claim cannot be sustained by any historical evidence.

[17] Technically, Constantine ruled over less than 20% of the world's population, but he did rule over the majority of Christians, therefore he was providentially well positioned to call a council that represented the majority of Christians.

Medieval Church (6th-14th centuries)

After the fall of the Roman Empire in the West, a power vacuum was created, which was gradually filled by the Bishop of Rome, for good and for ill. In a sense the Bishop of Rome had become a shadow of the emperor, residing in an imperial capital and naturally taking a prominent role in ecclesiastical affairs. After the emperor was gone, the Roman Bishop remained, and he gradually began to fill some of the pragmatic roles the emperor had in society.

This era also saw the dramatic conversions of Germanic "barbarians" in Western Europe. These barbarian cultures were extremely superstitious, even by Roman polytheistic standards, and their influence naturally lent itself to a much higher and much more superstitious form of sacerdotalism. During this early medieval period, sacerdotalism became hardcore.

In the 11th century the Roman Bishop began burning heretics and taking other measures to directly coerce faith. It is no accident that the schism between the Eastern and Western Church happened around this time. This was the true birth of the Papacy, and doctrinal justifications for it continued to develop over the next couple centuries. All of this culminated doctrinally when Pope Boniface VIII issued *Unam Sanctum* in 1302. Politically, however, his power was not universally accepted; in fact, it was his political struggle that motivated Boniface to make such outlandish claims in the first place. Nevertheless, the political power and influence of the Pope continued to grow in Europe, until the time of the Reformation. In short, the Western Church ended up with *papal sacerdotalism.*

The Eastern Church, meanwhile, developed along different ecclesiological lines. The Eastern half of the Roman Empire proved to be much more politically stable and never fell until the 15th century; consequently their church retained its Christian civil magistrate and never had occasion to develop anything like a papacy. Eastern Missionary outreaches to pagan Russia in the 9th century eventually resulted in the conversion of Vladimir I in the 10th century, and for most of their history the Russians have also retained an explicitly Christian magistrate.

Sacerdotalism in the East deepened over time, in much the same way it did in the West. Interestingly, the Eastern combination of magisterialism with extreme sacerdotalism caused them to 'sacralize' their emperors and civil magistrates to an unusual degree, with many of them ending up as canonized saints! To this day the Eastern Orthodox use the titles "Constantine Equal to the Apostles", "Vladimir Equal to the Apostles", etc.

Contrasted with the West, the Eastern Church saw a stronger emphasis on asceticism and the spiritual power of monks, with a few (like Simeon the New Theologian) controversially teaching that the special charisma of the bishops passed on to monks and monasteries. Monks have therefore played a more prominent role in Eastern Orthodoxy than in Roman Catholicism, which remains true even today. Setting aside charismatic monks though, the reins of power in Eastern Orthodoxy remained solidly with the bishops and the magistrates. Over the centuries they retained a self-conscious magisterial ecclesiology, despite marching deeper down the broad path of sacerdotalism. We can therefore accurately and succinctly describe their ecclesiology during this era as: *magisterial sacerdotalism.*

Reformation Era (15th-17th centuries)

During the Middle Ages the text of Scripture had been largely inaccessible, partly due to historical circumstance and partly by design. Obtaining a copy of the Bible was prohibitively expensive, and reading it in Latin or Greek required a level of literacy and linguistic training unavailable to most. To top it all off, the Roman Church punished men like Wycliffe who sought to translate and circulate the Scriptures. If the words of Scripture are water from heaven, then the Middle Ages were a pretty big drought.

The Reformation changed that. Early reformers like Jan Hus began to read Scripture, to translate it, and to circulate it more widely; and the more they did so, the more men began to reject errors like the Pope, icons, indulgences, transubstantiation, etc. Unfortunately none of these reforms really gained steam in Europe until the advent of the printing press. Before Gutenberg it is estimated there were perhaps 30,000 physical books present in all of Europe.[18] Texts and arguments and Scripture itself simply couldn't circulate quickly or widely enough. But after the printing press, a reformation of some kind became inevitable.

Nothing is more toxic to sacertodalism than pervasive reading of Scripture, thanks not only to its teachings, but also to the very act of reading itself. It's much harder to defend the notion of a priestly 'mediator' when readers have direct access to the words of God.

---

[18] Cf. "Gutenberg's Legacy," from the *Harry Ransom Center at The University of Texas at Austin*, accessed on May 17, 2017, http://www.hrc.utexas.edu/educator/modules/gutenberg/books/legacy/.)

In 1520 Luther published his three famous treatises (*On the Freedom of a Christian, The Babylonian Captivity of the Church,* and *Letter to the Christian Nobility*), reclaiming the doctrine of the universal priesthood of all believers and articulating the core of Protestantism. This was nothing less than the re-birth of historic evangelicalism, and a corresponding rejection of sacerdotalism and all its superstitious and corrupt entanglements. His treatises also sparked the rebirth of magisterialism in the West, with Luther directly appealing to civil magistrates to guard the church and providing clear arguments to back up his case.

During this era the anarchic evangelicals (anabaptists) also emerged. Though initially some were violent revolutionaries, they eventually settled down to become the secluded, peaceful schismatics that we know today. At the risk of oversimplifying, one could summarize the anabaptists as being driven by a radical interpretation of the Sermon on the Mount. They interpreted Jesus' commands to forgive criminals and to tolerate cheek-slapping as commands for outright pacifism. Consequently, there could be no room for civil justice anymore; the kingdom of the church must supersede all that. The result was an odd imitation of one key tenet of sacerdotalism, even amidst their fierce reaction to it: they too made the external visible community part of the *esse* of the church, rather than a manifestation of an identity hidden in Christ. By contrast, Luther placed the radical words of Jesus in their broader scriptural context and drew distinctions between the "two kingdoms," spiritual and temporal. Christians have one foot in this temporal kingdom of scarcity and penal justice, and one foot in the spiritual kingdom of God. The Sermon on the Mount speaks to the latter, giving commands that we Christians must obey as spiritual followers of Christ. Nevertheless, if a Viking horde invades our country to rape and pillage, then it is good for us *as citizens* to join the civil magistrate in defending the weak against such oppressors. Temporal justice requires it. This speaks to the temporal kingdom, which will remain with us until it passes away in the eschaton. Luther therefore explains that all Christians are dual-citizens, living in both the spiritual and temporal kingdoms, and each citizenship requires different duties of us. The anabaptists failed to draw these distinctions, preferring instead to deny (inconsistently) participation in the temporal realm.

Meanwhile in the Eastern Church, attempts at reformation largely failed. Constantinople had fallen to the Turks in 1453, and therefore Muslims ruled over the Eastern Christians for the entirety of the reformation era. The environment was not one conducive to theological change, but some attempted anyway. Cyril Lucaris (1572-1638) became persuaded of evangelicalism, and when he was appointed Ecumenical Patriarch of Constantinople he sought to reform the Eastern Orthodox church accordingly.[19] He sent theologians to study under Protestants in England and Geneva, and he oversaw the introduction of the first printing press in Greece with the goal of making the Scriptures more widely available (sadly, the press was confiscated shortly afterwards). Cyril was persecuted by both Romanists and Ottomans, and was ultimately murdered by the latter for political reasons. The attempted reforms of Cyril were controversial when he was alive, and

---

[19] To learn more about Cyril Lucaris, see George A. Hadjiantoniou *Protestant Patriarch: The Life of Cyril Lucaris, 1572-1638* (Richmond, VA: John Knox Press, 1961). .

after his death they were officially denounced by most other Eastern patriarchs and bishops at two synods.[20] The Eastern Church therefore remained staunchly sacerdotal.

THE SIGNIFICANCE OF MAGISTERIAL PROTESTANTISM

When we debate ecclesiology, the issue at stake is the very definition of Christianity itself. What is the church? What is our relationship to God and man? The two greatest commandments are to love God, and to love our neighbor. Magisterial Protestantism speaks to both of these in central ways.

Starting with the second commandment: Magisterialism concerns the way we go about loving our neighbor. Over against the papists, the doctrine of magisterialism and the two kingdoms enables us to explain clearly why faith may *not* be coerced. One of Luther's heresies that Pope Leo X ordered him to recant was, "That heretics be burned is against the will of the Spirit."[21] Luther famously responded to Leo's demands:

> Unless I am convinced by the testimony of the Holy Scriptures or by evident reason—for I can believe neither pope nor councils alone,

---

[20] After Cyril's death, some Eastern Orthodox bishops retroactively claimed that he had never advocated for such reforms, that it was all just a big misunderstanding, that his confession of faith was actually a forgery, etc. Reading Cyril's letters gives a much different impression and clearly reveals his commitment to evangelical principles. See *Lettres Anecdotes de Cyrille Lucar*, (Amsterdam: Chez L'Honoré et Chatelain, 1718).

[21] "Exsurge Domine," item 33, *Papal Encyclicals Online*, accessed August 15, 2016, http://www.papalencyclicals.net/Leo10/l10exdom.htm.

as it is clear that they have erred repeatedly and contradicted themselves—I consider myself convicted by the testimony of Holy Scripture, which is my basis; my conscience is captive to the Word of God. Thus I cannot and will not recant, because acting against one's conscience is neither safe nor sound. God help me. Amen.[22]

There's a reason we don't have inquisitions anymore. The religious freedom enjoyed in the Western world today is ultimately, through a long and complex process of development, a product of the Reformation's ecclesiology. We believe faith cannot be coerced, because the sword belongs to the civil magistrate and the temporal kingdom. In the same breath magisterialism allows us to explain, over against anabaptists, why *civil justice* in fact *should* be coerced. These are not just heady academic arguments: this is practical stuff. Bishops should not burn heretics, but the magistrate should punish criminals. It sounds obvious to say it that way, but it is our doctrine of the two kingdoms that sets the natural foundation for it.

Regarding the first commandment: Evangelicalism clarifies our direct relationship with God. We deny any fictitious mediators like priests on earth or demigod saints who receive our prayers in heaven. There is only one mediator between God and man, Christ Jesus.

Evangelical doctrine defines the church as the people of God, not as an institution or a hierarchical structure like Catholics and Orthodox believe. For Protestants, the church is not limited by the workings of man or his struc-

---
[22] Translated by Heiko Oberman in *Luther: Man Between God and the Devil* (New Haven: Yale University Press, 1989), 39.

37

tures. The church moves as the Holy Spirit moves in the hearts of men. Wherever men profess Christ, there the dominion of Christ's body reaches. The Kingdom of God is not a little tree growing in a pot, with people standing around arguing over how many trunks or branches it might have. The Kingdom of God is an expanding forest, a river flooding out uncontrollably.

Ultimately, sacerdotalists like Roman Catholics and Eastern Orthodox do not believe in the church. They believe in bishops. For them Jesus does not stand at the center of the church as the *sine qua non*. My local presbyterian church definitely has Jesus, but by their standards we do not have all that matters most for a church, because we don't have a bishop with apostolic succession. Ecclesiologically they place bishops at the center of the church, alongside Jesus. Two or more believers might gather together, but apparently they are only guaranteed to have the Holy Spirit in His fullness if they acknowledge the authority of a bishop.

In a sense, our ecclesiology points to what we value most. How do we define "the church"? Buildings? Written constitutions? Leaders that we call bishops? No. All those things might be good, but none of them define the center or the essence of the church. The definition of the church is *Christ*. Do you have faith in him? Do you follow him? Then you are part of the church. The church is Christ's body, not the body of a bunch of clergy. Faith in Jesus is of central importance.

In short: Protestant ecclesiology places Christ at the center.

PART II:
PROTESTANT ECCLESIOLOGY IN SCRIPTURE

III:

FINDING ZION: THE CHURCH
IN THE OLD TESTAMENT
Steven Wedgeworth

ANY contemporary student of Scripture assigned with the task of finding the Christian Church in the Old Testament will quickly throw up the white flag of traditional dogmatics. After all, "the church" is a New Testament creation. There are no uses of the term "church" in English translations of the Old Testament, and any attempt to use the Greek term *ekklesia* requires navigating the Septuagint and its layers of lexical, religious, and political history. Distinctively Christian, even sectarian, assumptions as to what the church is "all about" control what it is we think we are looking for when we search out the Old Testament. We look to the temple, the incipient synagogue system, or the nation of Israel, or we resist looking to any of these, because we have already defined "church" before reading the Old Testament.

In an effort to improve this situation, even if only partially, this essay will attempt to give us a better understanding of the nature of our question. What exactly is "the church" from the Old Testament's point of view? To this end, we will summarize the more recent historical attempts to locate "the church" in Old Testament socio-ecclesial structures, particularly the *qahal*. We will then compare that quest with other key Biblical-theological images and concepts that are often neglected in these investigations. Finally, we will highlight a few apparent points of dissonance in the Old Testament picture, as well as its eschatological imagery, all of which should have informed circumspect readers of ancient times of the need for some resolution or eschatological fulfillment to come.

READING BACKWARDS: *EKKLESIA AND QAHAL*

Within Protestantism, there have always been two poles regarding the definition of the church. The more "Lutheran" position emphasizes true faith as the essence of the church, and it is therefore reluctant to construct a church with fixed temporal boundaries.[1] Instead, "the church" is "the people of God," understood simply in the sense of actual believers gathered around a spiritual or charismatic manifestation of the word. The opposite emphasis, sometimes conceived of as "Presbyterian" and at other times as "High Church," prioritizes the external structure of the

---

[1] On this point see Jonathan D. Trigg's insightful work on baptism and ecclesiology in Martin Luther, *Baptism in the Theology of Martin Luther* (Leiden: Brill, 1994), 174-203. The challenge of holding this somewhat ethereal definition in harmony with the strong emphasis on the sacraments has, over the years, led to a reaction within Lutheranism, and one can find "high church" and "low church" parties there as in other traditions. In this section we must content ourselves with generalities. Amidst a summary of the "modern consensus" on defining the church, James Tunstead Burtchaell provides a quote from Rudolph Sohm which nicely summarizes the thoroughgoing "Lutheran" point of view in "Church law stands in contradiction to the essence of the church," in *From Synagogue to Church*, (Cambridge: Cambridge University Press, 1992), 87.

church to such an extent that it looks for historical institutions as constitutive of the church.

While some outside the bounds of Protestantism are content to claim that Jesus created the offices of the church *de novo*, most within Protestantism, particularly Reformed Protestantism, have preferred to see "the church" as a continuation of Israel and its polity. Thus they have looked to specific social and political structures within Israel as keys to identifying and defining Christian ecclesiastical law and government. This assumption tends to dominate one's study of the Old Testament, predisposing the reader to look for church government in the Torah or to locate the priesthood or the civil government as potential antecedents to "the church."

The most pervasive instance of this is somewhat generic, basing the office of "ruling elder" upon the tribal elders of the Old Testament. There were, however, other claims that were made about specific historical institutions, namely the Sanhedrin. It was John Calvin who identified the presbytery with the Jewish Sanhedrin,[2] and while Calvin did not fully resolve this with other aspects of his theology, he did make the claim that the Christian Church "maintained" the "order" which existed under the law.[3]

---

[2] *Commentary* on Matthew 18:16.

[3] Calvin claims that Jesus appealed to the Jewish model as an order that "was lawful and approved by God" and as something that was "handed down to them from the fathers." Calvin adds, "Yet there is no reason to doubt that the form of discipline, which prevailed in the kingdom of Christ, succeeded in the room of that ancient discipline," "what had been preserved under the Law Christ has conveyed to us, because we hold the same rank with the ancient fathers," and "He reminded us that the order, which had been formerly established in a holy manner under the Law, must be maintained in his *Church*" (*ibid*). Calvin elsewhere advocates the distinction between the visible and invisible church and even maintains that true believers have always been a remnant within

Later *de jure divino* Presbyterians[4] hardened this claim of institutional succession, even sometimes rooting the Sanhedrin in divine law, usually the instruction of Jethro in Exodus 18 and the 70 elders of Exodus 24:9.

As influential as these traditional explanations are, they have both received ample criticism over the years. More recent scholarship has provided a much more thorough understanding of the Old Testament and Intertestamental ecclesiastical structures.[5] Very few argue that the New Testament church is an actual continuation of any Old Testament institution, yet most do agree that there is a sort of continuation of key themes. The most common argument along these lines is that the New Testament term *ekklesia* was simply understood, among Jews, to be the way to express the Hebrew term *qahal*.[6] This means that the New Testament term *ekklesia* most naturally referred to the

---

the visible church (for instance, "But because a small and contemptible number are hidden in a huge multitude and a few grains of wheat are covered by a pile of chaff, we must leave to God alone the knowledge of his church, whose foundation is His secret election," *Institutes* 4.1.2, trans. Ford Lewis Battles and ed. John McNeil [Louisville, KY: Westminster Press, 1960], 2:1013). Calvin's emphasis on the visible church, and particularly its government, is what most distinguished "Reformed" ecclesiology from Lutheran, particularly as those traditions developed.

[4] *De jure divino* is a theological conviction regarding church government. The phrase means "of divine right," and those who subscribe to this position argue that there is one Biblically-commanded form of church government that is required for churches to be true churches.

[5] The survey in Burtchaell is especially helpful, 61-179.

[6] See for example, D. Douglas Bannerman, *The Scripture Doctrine of the Church Historically and Exegetically Considered* (Edinburgh: T&T Clark, 1887), 92-97; Walter Lowrie, *The Church and Its Organization In Primitive and Catholic Times* (New York: Longmans, Green, and Co, 1904), 104; Herman Bavinck, *Reformed Dogmatics* (Grand Rapids: Baker Academic, 2008), 4:277-279; Burtchaell, 209-215; and James D.G. Dunn *Jesus Remembered* (Grand Rapids: William B. Eerdmans, 2013), 513-14.

"assembly" of the people of God. The most prominent *qahal* in Jewish memory was the festival assembly at Sinai. It is important to note that the term could also carry a more occasional meaning, as it does in Ezekiel 27:34 and then again in the New Testament in Acts 19:32, though these would be exceptions determined to be such by their contexts. Still, there was a known concept of the assembly, and most scholars point out that the technical point of distinction for *qahal* was that it had a universal intent. When used in connection to the assembly of Israel, it did not refer to any one small-group gathering (not a "congregation") but rather all of the people, the entire nation. As such, in the New Testament, *ekklesia* would include all of the people of Jesus.[7]

When we look at the various uses of *qahal* in the Old Testament, we see the most pronounced instances in Exodus through Deuteronomy, the Solomonic period (especially 2 Chronicles), Ezra-Nehemiah, and Ezekiel. The overwhelming majority of instances refer to the calling together of Israel for a religious activity, though many of the uses in Ezekiel are actually in reference to various gatherings of the enemies of Israel (usually military units).

There is at least one case in the Psalms where *qahal* is applied to the heavenly assembly:

> And the heavens will praise Your wonders,
> O Lord;
> Your faithfulness also in the *assembly* of the
> saints.
> For who in the heavens can be compared to

---

[7] Douglas Bannerman writes that the term *qahal* "denotes properly the whole body of any people, united by common bonds in one society, and constituting some kind of republic or commonwealth" (90).

the Lord?
Who among the sons of the mighty can be
likened to the Lord?
God is greatly to be feared in the *assembly* of
the saints,
And to be held in reverence by
all those around Him. (Ps 89:5-7)

The idea that there is a heavenly *qahal* on which the earthly
one is modeled will become an important point for New
Testament theology. It is only hinted at here.[8]

What we also see from this and other uses is that
qahal is an activity, an *assembling* of people (or perhaps angels) around a civil or religious leader for an official purpose. It is very much connected to the etymology of *ekklesia*: those who are called out.

The nature of *qahal* in the Old Testament already
challenges easy assumptions that the church will have an
obvious institutional structure. It is one thing to claim to
be the historical successor to the Sanhedrin or the synagogue system. It does not make the same kind of sense to
speak that way about the *qahal*, especially when there has
been a change in the larger civic realm. Indeed, we see a
rather complicated relationship between the various teachers of the Torah, the temple leaders, the Sanhedrin, and
the civil magistrates in the gospel narratives.

---

[8] There has been a vast output of literature known as "temple theology"
which seeks to explain the way in which the Hebrews understood their
worship to relate to heavenly worship. See Margaret Barker, *The Gate of
Heaven* (Sheffield: Sheffield Phoenix Press, 2008); Margaret Barker, *Temple Theology: An Introduction* (London: SPCK, 2004); and *Heaven on Earth*,
ed. T. Desmond Alexander and Simon Gathercole (Carlisle: Paternoster,
2004). However, there has thus far not been an extensive connection of
this temple theology to the *qahal*.

THE CHURCH AS "HOUSE"

D. Douglas Bannerman, one of the sons of the more famous James Bannerman, points out that before *qahal* at-
tained regular usage, the primary description for the cove-
nanted people of God was simply "house" or "household."[9] Early on in Genesis we meet the household of Noah (Gen. 7:1), and it is important to remember that the
New Testament identifies the Ark-experience as a type of
the church (1 Peter 3:20-21). We then move on to the
house of Abraham, the house of Jacob, and, once Jacob
becomes a larger figure and takes his new name, the house
of Israel, each having a covenantal significance. The term
originally carried the meaning of family or dynasty, as in
Genesis 15:2-3 or Exodus 19:2.

We soon meet a second meaning of "house," the
more literal expression of a dwelling place. This is the primary meaning of "the house of God" when that phrase
occurs in the Old Testament. It is an altar, a tent, or a
temple. The expression "house of God" first appears in
Genesis 28:19, 22. We see the name and concept of
"house" expanded upon as God establishes a "tabernacle"
or a "tent" for His dwelling place (Ex. 25:8-8, 26:7). This
tabernacle is itself referred to as "the house of the LORD"
(Ex. 23:19, Josh. 6:24, 2 Sam. 12:20) or "the house of
God" (Judges 18:31, 1 Chron. 6:48), and it would eventually make its way into the temple.

Understanding this dual meaning of "house" in the
Old Testament can help us to see the temple and its ministry as broader than and, in some ways, distinguishable
from the sacerdotal cult. Obviously the temple and the

[9] Bannerman, 74-88.

Levitical ministry are intimately related, and yet it is still undeniable that the house of God is a theme which relates to dynasty and kingdom as much as it does the priesthood. For their part, the priesthood and the sacrificial system predate the temple and are said to have their own spiritual analogues (for instance, Ps. 51:17). This is significant for the long-standing opposition of a "temple model" to a "synagogue model" because, while there are certainly key differences, both, it would seem, also have key parallels to the New Testament church.

Perhaps the most interesting aspect of the "house" theme in the Old Testament is the famous Davidic covenant of 2 Samuel 7. The two meanings of family and dwelling-place are united in the promise made to David, and it is God Himself who brings them together. This dual meaning of "house," then is also related to the temple, since the play on the meaning of "house" made by God is itself a response to David's desire to build the temple:

> Would you build a house for Me to dwell in? For I have not dwelt in a house since the time that I brought the children of Israel up from Egypt, even to this day, but have moved about in a tent and in a tabernacle. Wherever I have moved about with all the children of Israel, have I ever spoken a word to anyone from the tribes of Israel, whom I commanded to shepherd My people Israel, saying, "Why have you not built Me a house of cedar?"

> ...When your days are fulfilled and you rest with your fathers, I will set up your seed after you, who will come from your body, and I will establish his kingdom. He shall build a house for My name, and I will establish the

> throne of his kingdom forever. I will be his
> Father, and he shall be My son. If he commits
> iniquity, I will chasten him with the rod of
> men and with the blows of the sons of
> men. But My mercy shall not depart from
> him, as I took it from Saul, whom I removed
> from before you. And your house and your
> kingdom shall be established forever before
> you. Your throne shall be established forever.
> (2 Sam. 7:5-7, 12-16)[10]

There is an important play on words in this passage. David will not build God a house, but instead God will build David a house. This "house" is a family dynasty, represented by Solomon, his offspring. But intriguingly, it will be from that family succession (that "house") that the temple (God's "house") will be built: "He shall build a house for My name…."

To only read this as a reference to Solomon's building of the temple, however, misses an important layer to the rhetorical play. Solomon will indeed build a literal house for God, but Solomon's dynasty, his family "house," will also be the earthly line for God's Son. "He shall build a house for my name, and I will establish the throne of his kingdom forever. I will be his Father, and he shall be My Son." Solomon's son will be God's son. Solomon's family will be God's family. Solomon's house will be God's house.

The Christian interpretation of the everlasting Davidic kingdom is that it is indeed the kingdom of the Son of God, the kingdom of Jesus Christ. The "house" that Solomon builds for God is the literal temple as well as the

---

[10] All scriptural references are to the New King James Version unless otherwise noted.

line of Christ. The "throne" that is established forever comes through the familial descent of David, and so David's house and God's house culminate in the same point, the messianic heir. Jesus is David's son and David's lord.

While exegetes and theologians alike rightly stress the distinction between "church" and "kingdom," it seems that the use of "house" in the Old Testament, especially David's house, necessarily brings them together on an important level. Douglas Bannerman also points out the relevance of this association when Jesus says that He will "build" His *ekklesia*. Bannerman quotes Hermann Cremer saying, "When Christ says, *oikodomeso mou ten ekklesian* ['I will build my *ekklesia*'], we are scarcely reminded that *ekklesia* denoted in profane Greek the place of assembly as well as the assembly itself, but rather that the Old Testament community was 'the House of Israel.'"[11] Jesus was building an assembly when He built His church. He was also building a house.

OTHER SQUARE PEGS

In addition to the two concepts of assembly and house, there are other complicating factors in finding the church in the Old Testament. Prior to the establishment of the priestly and tabernacle ministry, there are various people who are both priests and kings. Melchizedek is the most famous, thanks to his significance in the New Testament, and, it is important to note, Melchizedek is offered as a superior type of priestly order (Hebrews 5:5-11, 6:20-7:25) to that of Levi and, therefore, to the Aaronic line and the Mosaic covenant. Melchizedek is not alone in this dual

---

[11] Bannerman, 95.

office, however, as Noah, Abraham, and Jacob also carry priestly and princely prerogatives. In fact, Jethro appears to also be this sort of priest-king, as he is explicitly identified as a "priest of Midian" (Ex. 2:16, 3:1). Yet, importantly, Jethro is also the owner of the flock of sheep which Moses tends in Ex. 3:1, and Jethro instructs Moses in clearly political matters in Ex. 18, when he gives advice on how to arrange a system of varying jurisdictions and subsidiarity.

Whether or not Jethro was a priest-king like those in the book of Genesis, one thing is certain about him. He was a Gentile. The existence of a gentile priest after the establishment of the tabernacle[12] is fascinating and stretches the boundaries of the Old Testament "church." Indeed, this is the sort of arrangement that would not be possible in the fully-formed conception of the New Testament church. Any true believer would be a member, by definition, and yet, in Exodus, Jethro is both a true believer and someone who is very much outside Israel and its assemblies.

Jethro is not the only believing Gentile depicted in the Old Testament. Hiram, king of Tyre, certainly seems like a believer when the text says that he "had always loved David" (1 Kings 5:1). He then offers to help finance the temple, saying "Blessed be the LORD this day, for He has given David a wise son over this great people!" (1 Kings 5:7ff). The recording of this event in 2 Chronicles is even more pronounced (2 Chron. 2:11-15). We also see important believing Gentiles in the Elijah-Elisha narrative.

---

[12] Note that in Exodus 18:27 Jethro went "to his own land." We are given no indication that he should have joined Israel instead, and based upon his confession in vs. 10-12, we have every reason to believe that Jethro returned to Midian as a priest of the true God.

Jesus Himself highlights the fact that the widow of Zarephath and Naaman were Gentiles (Luke 4:25-27). When we look at these characters in their Old Testament contexts, we can see that they are portrayed as becoming believers in Israel's God (1 Kings 17:24, 2 Kings 5:14-18). This theme of believing Gentiles will also loom large in the prophets, where the conversion of Gentiles is both a sign of judgment against Israel and a sign of the restored kingdom and of the new heavens and the new earth. Certain high-profile Gentile kings like Nebuchadnezzar, Darius, and Cyrus[13] are all presented as believers in Israel's God.

What this means is that, if we assume a broad concept of "all believing persons" in our definition of the church as "the people of God," the Old Testament actually presents a "church" that is considerably broader than Israel. There were believers in the true God prior to the formation of Israel as a distinct people who were never subsumed by Israel, and there were Gentiles converted by Israel who remained outside of Israel. If we restrict our definition of the church to a notion of *qahal*, then these Gentiles appear to be outside of the church. However, if we broaden our definition of the church to something like "all believers as such," then these believing Gentiles would lead us to reconsider our understanding of what makes something a *qahal* (perhaps it is possible to have a *qahal* outside of Israel's national boundaries as in Psalm 89 mentioned above) or to simply affirm a significant discontinuity between the Old and New Covenant on the relationship between salvation and the church.

---

[13] Darius and Cyrus may well be the same person.

ZION AND THE TABERNACLE OF DAVID

Another significant challenge to any institutional definition of the church in the Old Testament is the role of the Davidic tabernacle and its counterpart in various prophetic utterances, Mt. Zion (Psalm 48, Is. 2:1-4, Zech. 8:1-5). David already stretches the limits of the priestly system in key places. Jesus highlights David's eating of the showbread (Matt. 12:3-4), but David, himself not a Levitical priest, engaged in other priestly actions as well. When David brought the ark to Jerusalem, the text says that he was "wearing a linen ephod" (2 Sam. 6:14), a priestly garment. Immediately following the procession into Jerusalem and the erection of the tabernacle, David "offered burnt offerings and peace offerings before the LORD" and then "blessed the people in the name of the LORD of hosts" (2 Sam. 6:17-18).

It is in the tabernacle of David where we see an even more curious challenge to our search for "the church" in the Old Testament, as it plays a unique and provocative role in the development of God's dwelling place. Peter Leithart, in his excellent *From Silence to Song*, has explored this particular issue in detail, giving an extended study of the tabernacle of David and its role in Israel's redemptive history. He points out that this tabernacle was actually distinct from the Mosaic tabernacle and that it was the Davidic tabernacle which was "the only place of worship ever set up on Zion."[14] He goes on to argue that while "Zion terminology and symbolism was transferred to the temple mount," the temple mount was not actually mount Zion,

---

[14] Leithart, *From Silence to Song: The Davidic Liturgical Revolution* (Moscow, ID: Canon Press, 2003), 13.

and there were important ways in which the Davidic tabernacle still retained precedence throughout the prophetic writings.[15] Indeed, Amos 9:11 states that God will "rebuild the tabernacle of David," and the New Testament claims that this is fulfilled in the Christian church (Acts 15:16).

Zion, the actual geographical location of David's tabernacle, attains an immensely important standing in the prophetic literature,[16] and it is Zion more than any other name which the prophets hold up as an eschatological ideal of the worldwide kingdom of God. One key example appears in two places in the prophets:

> Now it shall come to pass in the latter days
> That the mountain of the Lord's house
> Shall be established on the top of the mountains,
> And shall be exalted above the hills;
> And peoples shall flow to it.
> Many nations shall come and say,
> "Come, and let us go up to the mountain of the Lord,
> To the house of the God of Jacob;
> He will teach us His ways,
> And we shall walk in His paths."
> For out of Zion the law shall go forth,
> And the word of the Lord from Jerusalem.
> He shall judge between many peoples,
> And rebuke strong nations afar off;
> They shall beat their swords into plowshares,
> And their spears into pruning hooks;
> Nation shall not lift up sword against nation,
> Neither shall they learn war anymore. (Micah 4:1-3; cf. Isaiah 2:2-4)

---

[15] Leithart, 73.

[16] Leithart explores this theme at length, 73-100.

A few points deserve noting here. The eschatological mountain, full of so much Biblical-theological significance, is identified as the "LORD's house." Thus it is a vision of the temple. But, as we have seen, it is also the continuing line of God's people. This mountain attracts Gentiles, who "flow to it" in order to receive the law. This law comes "out of Zion," and it then establishes God's rule across the world. This new worldwide order of blessing is the eschatological Zion.

Zechariah 8 also speaks of Zion. There we see that Zion is "in the midst of Jerusalem" (Zech. 8:3). As it happens, when David conquered Zion, it was the central stronghold or fortress (2 Sam. 5:6-10, 2 Chron. 11:4-7). David "built the city around it" (2 Chron. 11:8). Thus when the prophets speak of "the city of David" and "the city of Zion," there are literal referents in Israel's history. The literal Zion was the location of David's tabernacle, and this Zion will be the New Jerusalem.

As we mentioned a little earlier, Acts 15:16 claims that the tabernacle of David was restored in the Christian church. The incorporation of Gentiles into the assembly of Jesus is a fulfillment of Amos' prophecy about David's tabernacle. In addition to this, Mt. Zion is also named in relation to the church in the New Testament. This happens in the famous passage from Hebrews 12:

> For you have not come to the mountain that may be touched and that burned with fire, and to blackness and darkness and tempest, and the sound of a trumpet and the voice of words, so that those who heard it begged that the word should not be spoken to them anymore (For they could not endure what was commanded: "And if so

> much as a beast touches the mountain, it shall be stoned or shot with an arrow." And so terrifying was the sight that Moses said, "I am exceedingly afraid and trembling." But you have come to Mount Zion and to the city of the living God, the heavenly Jerusalem, to an innumerable company of angels, to the general assembly and church of the firstborn who are registered in heaven, to God the Judge of all, to the spirits of just men made perfect, to Jesus the Mediator of the new covenant, and to the blood of sprinkling that speaks better things than that of Abel. (Heb. 12:18-24)

This is a rich passage with several noteworthy terms and ideas, all of which attain fuller significance in light of the Old Testament material. Clearly the concept of the *qahal* is in play. The Sinai assembly is referenced as the Old Covenant counterpart to what the New Covenant people are now coming to. Their new *qahal*, it is worth noting, is also a mountain assembly. It is "Mount Zion," the heavenly city of eschatological hope. The term *ekklesia* is also included, thus filling out the picture. The new mountain we have come to is a church.

Of course, the Hebrews text cannot simply be applied to the polity of a local congregation. This city is heavenly, after all, and the assembly includes angels as well as saints who have lived before. The author of Hebrews is showing us the invisible and eschatological reality that the Christian church encounters, and it is speaking objectively. This is the reality that Christians "come to" in light of the work of Christ and the giving of the Holy Spirit. As we understand the relationship between Zion and the Tabernacle of David and combine it with the fact that Acts 15 has identified the Tabernacle of Zion with the incorporation of the Gentiles into the Christian community, then we see that the activity happening within the believers is itself eschatological. When the people gather together, they manifest that the "house of David" has been built. Through their union with Christ and in the indwelling of the Holy Spirit, they are both the kingdom and his sanctuary. They are the tabernacle of David and the house for his name.

This has momentous significance for the *qahal* in the New Testament, which is to say, for the church. In context, the Hebrews passage is not restricted to a ceremonial liturgical gathering. It is describing the Christian life as such. Hebrews 12 begins with a meditation on suffering and then moves on to commend peacemaking and holy living. Chapter 13 extols hospitality and praises marriage. Thus the eschatological "church" is given as a foundation for the whole of the life of sanctification. Because we have come to God's holy mountain and heavenly city, we must pursue peace and holiness (Heb. 12:14), we must avoid bitterness which can produce fornication (Heb. 12:15-16), we must not refuse to hear God's voice (Heb. 12:25-26), and we must serve God acceptably with reverence and fear (Heb. 12:28). This last expression certainly denotes worship, as it uses *latreuomen*, but the larger context of the passage, particularly chapters 11 and 12 taken together, is of the Christian life of faithfulness as a whole with a special emphasis on persevering over a lifetime.

CONCLUSION

In many ways, this study has attempted to complicate the question of the church in the Old Testament. There is no singular Old Testament institution which fully encapsulates the church. The church brings together aspects of various Old Testament concepts, and it breaks the rules of several of those concepts along the way. As such, it is not possible to identify any one of Israel's social or political structures as being "the church." Many of those structures were themselves prophesied to be restored in new ways, ways which would thoroughly transform them.

However, having pointed out these challenges, a general consistency also appears. The church in the Old Testament is both the assembling of God's people together to hear His word, and the formation of His house, creating His family, His dwelling place, and His kingdom. This assembly is truly universal, as it includes all kinds of peoples, Jew and Gentile alike; it even unites heaven and earth. Fully understood, the church is a meeting with God Himself through the eschatological work of the messiah which then transforms the totality of the created order.

IV:

EXCURSUS: WHAT IS THE "CHURCH"? ETYMOLOGY AND CONCEPT IN CLASSICAL ANTIQUITY, THE LXX, AND THE NEW TESTAMENT

E.J. Hutchinson

THE ENGLISH and Greek words for "church" are etymologically unrelated, a fact that can go some way toward obscuring the force of the "church" concept in the New Testament. The English term is derived from the Greek *kuriakon* ("belonging to the Lord"), probably a shortening of the phrase *kuriakon doma*, "the Lord's house." Already, if we are not careful, we will begin to think of such things as buildings, and this will get us off on entirely the wrong foot.[1]

The word for "church" in the Greek New Testament, on the other hand, is *ekklesia*, which is derived from the verb *ekkalein*, "to call out." Thus the primary accent in the

---

[1] In addition to standard lexica and concordances, F.H. Jacobson's article "Church, The Christian," in Samuel Macauley Jackson (ed.), *The New Schaff-Herzog Encyclopedia of Religious Knowledge*, vol. 3, 77-85 (Grand Rapids, MI: Baker, 1952), was of great use in the preparation of this brief *excursus*.

New Testament, already in the term itself, rests on God's action in calling a people to himself. At the same time, the term has a social aspect as well: its meaning in classical Greek is "assembly." The New Testament use of the term, moreover, evokes resonances not only of the New Testament's cultural *milieu*, but also of Old Testament contexts in which the term is used in the Septuagint, the Greek translation of the Hebrew Bible. When thinking about what the "church" is, therefore, Christians would do well to have a general sense of the use of the term in these three contexts in mind—that is, the classical, LXX, and New Testament contexts.

We begin with the classical world and the use of *ekklesia* to mean "assembly." For instance, Aristotle, speaking of the heroes at Troy, writes: "The kingly office is in truth a kind of generalship, sovereign and perpetual. The king has not the power of life and death, except in certain cases, as for instance, in ancient times, he had it when upon a campaign, by right of force. This custom is described in Homer. For Agamemnon puts up with it when he is attacked in the assembly [*ekklesia*], but when the army goes out to battle he has the power even of life and death" (*Politics* 1285a7-12, tr. B. Jowett, rev. by S. Everson). In the New Testament, too, the word is employed to refer to different types of public assemblies in general (see Acts 19:32, 39, 41). But already in this passage of Aristotle we get a sense that in classical Greek the term most frequently means, not just any assembly, but a *political* assembly, or, as Liddell-Scott-Jones (*LSJ*, the standard classical Greek lexicon) puts it, an "assembly duly called"—one recalls the role of Achilles in *summoning* the people to assembly (*agoren...kalessato*) in *Iliad* 1 as Apollo's plague raged. Thus

Thucydides differentiates the *ekklesia* from the more general *sullogos* ("assembly, meeting") in *Peloponnesian War* 2.22, as *LSJ* points out: "But [Pericles], seeing that they were overcome by the irritation of the moment and inclined to evil counsels, and confident that he was right in refusing to go out, would not summon an assembly [*ekklesia*] or meeting [*sullogon*] of any kind, lest, coming together more in anger than in prudence, they might take some false step" (tr. B. Jowett). Because of this more precise meaning of the word, it is not surprising that the political body of assembled citizens in ancient Athens was called simply the *Ekklesia* (see Aristotle, *Constitution of Athens* 43).

This general sense of the word carries over into the Greek Old Testament, where *ekklesia*, rendering the Hebrew word *qahal*, is frequently used for the politico-religious Israelite congregation. It should be noted, however, that *qahal* is not always translated as *ekklesia*: for instance, it is translated as *synagoge* in Lev. 4:13-14. It should be further noted that *qahal* is not the only word for the "assembly" or "congregation," for which the term *edah*— never translated as *ekklesia*, but rather as *synagoge*—was also used. So, for instance, in Deut. 9:10 it refers to God's people as constituted and gathered by and around God's Word to them: "And the Lord gave me the two tablets of stone written with the finger of God, and on them were all the words that the Lord had spoken with you on the mountain out of the midst of the fire on the day of the assembly [*ekklesia*]."[2] Again, in 1 Sam. 17:46-47 the *ekklesia*

---

[2] For convenience, I use the *ESV* as the base-text for English translations herein and modify where necessary to reflect the usage of the LXX.

is the assembly of the special people of the Lord, not as gathered on a particular occasion for worship :

> This day the Lord will deliver you into my hand, and I will strike you down and cut off your head. And I will give the dead bodies of the host of the Philistines this day to the birds of the air and to the wild beasts of the earth, that all the earth may know that there is a God in Israel, and that all this assembly [*ekklesia*] may know that the Lord saves not with sword and spear. For the battle is the Lord's, and he will give you into our hand.

On the other hand, the term *can* be used precisely for such a gathering, as it is in Psalm 22:22: "I will tell of your name to my brothers; in the midst of the congregation [*ekklesia*] I will praise you." Or, again, with reference to Solomon's blessing at the dedication of the temple: "Then the king turned around and blessed all the assembly [*ekklesia*] of Israel, while all the assembly [*ekklesia*] of Israel stood" (2 Chron. 6.3). And shortly thereafter: "Then Solomon stood before the altar of the Lord in the presence of the assembly [*ekklesia*] of Israel and spread out his hands" (2 Chron. 6.12).

Nevertheless, because the blessing just mentioned is given by the king, we are reminded that the "worshipping" aspect of the people is not divorced from the "political" aspect of the people, even if at times one or the other element is foregrounded. In contrast, Nehemiah 5:7 emphasizes the "political" or judicial aspect of God's people: "I took counsel with myself, and I brought charges against the nobles and the officials. I said to them, 'You are exacting interest, each from his brother.' And I held a great assembly [*ekklesia*] against them...."

It is both curious and significant that when the writers of the New Testament sought a term for the assembly of believers in the resurrection of Jesus, they fixed not upon *synagoge* but instead on *ekklesia*. Why was this? Did it come to them directly from heathen political practice, or as mediated through the usage of the LXX? Given the background and concerns of the Apostles, there can be no doubt that the latter is correct. One might suggest, then, that the reason for their preference for one term over the other had a good deal to do with the particular resonances of that term, that is, with the idea that the assembly of God's people is the result of God's prior action; it is only convened as God himself "calls out" a people by his Word.

Already we find evidence of this in the title given to the assembly in the Pentateuch: "No one born of a forbidden union may enter the assembly of the Lord [*ekklesia kuriou*]. Even to the tenth generation, none of his descendants may enter the assembly of the Lord [*ekklesia kuriou*]" (Deut. 23:2). Compare also Judges 20:2: "And the chiefs of all the people, of all the tribes of Israel, presented themselves in the assembly of the people of God [*ekklesia tou laou tou theou*], 400,000 men on foot that drew the sword." Why is the assembly the "assembly of the Lord" or the "assembly of the people of God"? Because it ultimately rests on God's summoning. This relation of the creature to the creator, of being summoned from non-being to being and to life, is already evident in the opening chapter of Genesis: "And God called [*ekalesen*] the light day and he called [*ekalesen*] the darkness night. And evening came into existence [*egeneto*] and morning came into existence [*egeneto*], the first day" (Gen. 1.5). This pattern is continued in the life of Abraham, the man of promise and of faith. As he is about to sacrifice his only son, seemingly invalidated the promise of God with respect to his offspring, the angel of the Lord calls to him: "But the angel of the Lord called [*ekalesen*] to him from heaven and said, 'Abraham, Abraham!' And he said, 'Here am I.' He said, 'Do not lay your hand on the boy or do anything to him'" (Gen. 22:11-12). Almost immediately there follows a confirmation of the promises of God: "And the angel of the Lord called to Abraham a second time from heaven and said, 'By myself I have sworn, declares the Lord, because you have done this and have not withheld your son, your only son, I will surely bless you, and I will surely multiply your offspring as the stars of heaven and as the sand that is on the seashore'" (Gen. 22:15-16). This pattern is continued in the life of Israel: "Wherefore Israel was an infant, and I loved him, and out of Egypt I called back [*metekalesa*] his children" (Hosea 11:1).

This last passage is familiar from the Gospel of Matthew, but it is quoted in a different form: "Out of Egypt I called [*ekalesa*] my son" (Matt. 2:15). Here, of course, it refers to Christ, and thus we have found the key. The promises of the Lord to Abraham and his offspring are all "Yes" and "Amen" in the heir of the promise, the Lord Jesus Christ. As God fulfills his promises in Christ, he continues to call a people to himself: "I have not come to call [*kalesai*] the righteous but sinners to repentance" (Luke 5:32). This calling of a people through faith and repentance, and its concomitant promise of salvation, is taken up and continued by the Apostles, for "Peter said to them, 'Repent and be baptized every one of you in the name of Jesus Christ for the forgiveness of your sins, and you will receive the gift of the Holy Spirit. For the promise is for you and for your children and for all who are far off, everyone whom the Lord our God calls [*proskalesetai*] to himself" (Acts 2:38-39). Thus do sinners become the children of God.

And what is this new people? It is the "church," the *ekklesia*, the assembly of the redeemed. This is given summary form perhaps nowhere better than in the opening verses of 1 Corinthians:

> Paul, called [*kletos*] by the will of God to be an apostle of Christ Jesus, and our brother Sosthenes, to the church of God [*ekklesia tou theou*] that is in Corinth, to those sanctified in Christ Jesus, called [*kletois*] to be saints together with all those who in every place call upon [*epikaloumenois*] the name of our Lord Jesus Christ, both their Lord and ours: Grace to you and peace from God our Father and the Lord Jesus Christ. (1 Cor. 1.1-3)

Ekklesia tou theou is precisely the title often used for God's people in the Old Testament, here clarified as those who have been called by God in Christ and who call upon him in return. This—and not organizational structure, institutional authority, or anything else—is, most fundamentally, what the "church" is. This fact explains why Paul needs to add to "the church of God" the specification "that is in Corinth": the "church" is not in the first instance a particular local group—like a polis or city-state—nor is it a bureaucratically-systematized denominational federation. It transcends all such trappings that belong to common earthly life, for the "church" in its most basic sense—the called and the calling—is radically related by grace through faith to the ascended Christ, who has gone up on high, leading captivity captive and giving to his people the gift of his heavenly Spirit.

Are there implications in this concept for the organizational structure institutional authority of the local and regional church? Of course. But none of these constitute what the church is. At its most basic, the concept "church" is so simple that it can almost be missed as we hasten along to talk about what we sometimes consider to be more sophisticated, meaningful aspects of the doctrine, with polysyllabic words such as "ecclesiology." In the end, it is nothing more—and, much more significantly, nothing less—than the people constituted by God's summoning before the throne of Jesus Christ through his Word and Spirit, and their humble response to that call in repentance and faith.

V:

PENTECOST AS ECCLESIOLOGY

Alastair Roberts

AS SOURCES for our ecclesiology, the narrative portions of Scripture may be deemed relatively unpromising, especially when compared to the New Testament epistolary literature. Yet much of the New Testament teaching concerning the Church occurs first in the form of narrative, only later to be articulated in the form of theological exposition. The apostolic doctrine of the Church finds its grounding first in historical events, rather than being primarily a matter of abstract theologizing: the ecclesiology of the epistles is firmly founded upon God's acts in time and space.

Of all of the important passages in this context, the account of Pentecost in Acts 2 is the most foundational. From this and related texts, a rich ecclesiology *in nuce* can be developed. Within this article, I will explore some of this passage's latent possibilities for the doctrine of the Church before demonstrating some ways in which certain questions that attend our ecclesiology can be addressed from the book of Acts.

The Day of Pentecost occurs at the grand confluence of several streams of biblical narrative development, combining their forces into a mighty torrent of spiritual power. Discerning the direction of its course is one of the tasks to which this article is devoted. I will begin by charting some of its principal tributaries, before turning to the question of its movement downstream.

OVERCOMING THE DIVISION OF THE NATIONS

In Genesis 11, humanity is undivided, all speaking a single "lip" (a word that possibly has religious connotations, cf. Isaiah 19:18; Zephaniah 3:9) and a single speech (verse 1). They settle in the plain of Shinar where, forming and firing bricks and using asphalt for mortar, they undertake a vast building project, constructing a city and a tower whose top reaches the heavens. Within this megacity, with the immense tower as its religious heart, humanity would be preserved from being spread throughout the earth as God had intended it to be. Frustrating the builders of Babel's hubristic designs to a hegemonic universal world order, God descended from heaven and confused their lip, so that they could no longer understand each other (verses 5-7). Forced to abandon their building project—*Babel*—humanity is scattered abroad across the face of the entire earth.

Reading the account of Pentecost in Acts 2 against the foil of Babel is illuminating. The builders of Babel sought to construct a tower to ascend to the heavens, yet God descended to confuse their lip. The immediate and crucial backdrop to Pentecost is the ascension of Christ into the heavens (Acts 2:32-33), after which God descends in the Spirit at Pentecost to give the disciples the power of prophetic speech in a multitude of "tongues".

Babel was the moment when humanity was divided into many nations under judgment; this event provides the narrative context for the calling of Abraham as the one through whom all of the nations would be blessed (Genesis 12:1-3). At Pentecost many nations are brought together in the new "building project" of the Church. Although speaking many tongues, those tongues now express a single religious "lip" (cf. Zephaniah 3:9), as divine prophecy is given in many languages and dialects, not only in the religious tongue of Hebrew. The diversity of humanity becomes a vehicle for its religious unity and the era of the exclusivity of Hebrew is ended. By implication, Pentecost is a definitive and seminal moment in the fulfilment of the promise that all of the nations would be blessed in Abraham.

Throughout the rest of the New Testament, the out-working of Pentecost as the unification of the nations is a prominent theme. In Galatians 3:14, Paul makes explicit what the blessing of Abraham was—"the promise of the Spirit"—something that is implicit in the events of Pentecost. Elsewhere, in passages such as Ephesians 2–3, Paul prominently reflects upon God's establishment of a new building within which Gentiles and Jews are united on an equal footing.

THE GIFT OF THE SPIRIT

Several weeks after the Passover and the departure from Egypt, Israel arrived at Mount Sinai. In Exodus 19 and the chapters that follow, Israel assembles at Mount Sinai, where they see a theophanic manifestation of the Lord's power and glory. Moses ascends on top of the mountain, where he is given the Law by the Lord; he then brings the Law down to give it to all of the people. Sinai, however, is a site of national apostasy. The people and the newly designated high priest, Aaron, construct and worship the golden calf. Moses summons the Levites to himself, who slay three thousand rebels, after which they are set apart to guard and serve the tabernacle (Exodus 32:25-29).

There are several themes of Sinai to be seen in Acts 2. Explicit associations between the timing of the Feast of Pentecost and the Sinai event can already be found in the *Book of Jubilees*, a century or two before Christ. *Jubilees* connects Pentecost with other great covenant events, such as the covenant with Noah and Abram. More generally, much as Sinai is the constitutive event for the people following the Passover and the Exodus from Egypt, so Pentecost is the constitutive event for the Church, following the "exodus" of Christ's death and resurrection (cf. Luke 9:31).

At Pentecost, the anointed leader ascends on high, and is given the fundamental reality by which the covenant people's life will be ordered: Moses is given the Law, Christ is given the Spirit. There are theophanic manifestations reminiscent of Sinai—a heavenly sound as of a rushing mighty wind and divided tongues of flame. Various Second Temple Jewish and early rabbinic writers connected the flames and the voices of the Sinai theophany, regarding the flashes as a "visible" voice, which was in turn related to the inscription of the Law.[1] Some even spoke of the division of the flames in this context, relating it to seventy tongues of the nations or to the distinct words of the Law.[2]

---

[1] Cf. Exodus 20:18, they "saw" the voices and the flashes. Abraham Joshua Heschel, *Heavenly Torah: As Refracted Through the Generations*, ed. and trans. Gordon Tucker (London: Continuum, 2006), 294-95. Sejin Park, *Pentecost and Sinai: The Festival of Weeks as a Celebration of the Sinai Event* (London: T & T Clark, 2008), 213-14.

[2] *Pentecost and Sinai*, 213-14.

The tabernacle was established at Sinai and the Church is established as a new Temple at Pentecost as the divine glory presence descends upon it and the Church is "lit" as if a great lampstand (cf. Revelation 1:12-20). Elsewhere in the New Testament, both the Church and its individual members are presented as new temples of the Holy Spirit and a royal priesthood (1 Corinthians 3:17; 6:19; Ephesians 2:19-22; 1 Peter 2:4-5, note the echoes of Exodus 19:6). Whereas three thousand were slain at Sinai by the Levites, three thousand were "cut to the heart" at Pentecost, by those who would be set apart for a new ministry.

The verbal ambivalence of the term *glossa* ("tongue") in Acts 2 is noteworthy, referring to both speech and flame, exploring the same conjunction of imagery that is encountered elsewhere in writings of the period. The divine "word" descends in distributed flame upon the disciples, who proceed to deliver it in distributed languages.

Reflecting upon these images, we see a Church that is formed by the descent of the divine word upon it in the power of the Spirit, in an event redolent of Sinai. Whereas the tablets of the Law were the site where the divine word was once inscribed, now the fire of divine speech descends upon the disciples.[3] The constitution of the new covenant people through the inscription of the Law upon their hearts and the contrast between the economy of the Law and the economy of the Spirit are themes that pervade the New Testament, in fulfilment of Old Testament promise (Jeremiah 31:31-34; Ezekiel 36:26-27).

---

[3] The prophet is occasionally presented as the bearer of the fire of the divine word: Isaiah 6:6-7; Jeremiah 5:14; Revelation 11:5.

PROPHETIC SUCCESSION

I have already drawn attention to the importance of the event of Christ's Ascension as the narrative backdrop for the events of the Day of Pentecost. The relationship between the two events may be more apparent when we read Acts in conversation with 2 Kings 2. In that chapter, Elijah ascends into heaven. However, the ascension of Elijah is the "pentecost" of Elisha, as Elisha receives the firstborn portion of Elijah's spirit (2 Kings 2:9-15), a fact immediately demonstrated as Elisha repeats the miraculous division of the waters of the Jordan that Elijah had just performed with his mantle. This event is, in turn, reminiscent of Moses' passing of his leadership of Israel to Joshua on the far side of the Jordan, after which Joshua also entered the land through a miraculous parting of the River Jordan. It foreshadows in various ways the passing of John the Baptist's ministry to Christ at Christ's baptism in the Jordan.

Joshua, Elisha, and the disciples had all formerly served as apprentices, until they were charged and equipped to take up and continue the prophetic ministry of their masters. In 1 Kings 19:15-16, Elijah had been commissioned with a task, which he didn't finish before his ascension. Rather, Elisha completed Elijah's ministry in Elijah's spirit. The ascension of Christ would have brought Elijah's ascension to mind, as it was the only other closely comparable prior event. The wording of Luke 24:49, which charges the disciples to wait until they are "clothed" (*endusesthe*) with power from on high, may well have recalled this: the Spirit is the descending mantle of Jesus, the great Prophet.

Pentecost is spoken of as the "baptism" of the Holy Spirit (cf. Acts 1:5). In its placement within the wider structure of the book of Acts and also in the details of the narrative, it is closely congruent with the baptism of Jesus by John the Baptist as recorded in Luke. In Luke 3:21-22, as Jesus prays, the Spirit descends with physical phenomena and a sound from heaven, anointing and filling him for his prophetic ministry. In the chapter that follows, Jesus speaks of himself as anointed for the preaching of the gospel (Luke 4:18-19). The baptism of the Church at Pentecost is homologous with Christ's baptism at the Jordan: both are set apart for and thrust out upon their mission. The reception of the Spirit is also a token of sonship (cf. Luke 3:22): as the Church receives the Spirit, its members are marked out as the sons of God.[4]

Once again, these are fundamental themes of New Testament ecclesiology. In the ministry of the Church, the ascended Christ continues to work, albeit in a transformed manner: the Church's activity is in the power of his Spirit. Through the Spirit, the Church participates in Christ's status, as we are identified as beloved sons and daughters, and charged to act in his name.

---

[4] There are also kingdom themes, which I lack space to develop here. Just as the Spirit descends upon Saul as he is first marked out for the throne, making him a new man and causing him to prophesy (1 Sam. 10:5-6, 10-13), so the Spirit's descent upon the Church at Pentecost should be related to Christ's gift of a kingdom (cf. Luke 22:29-30). See Alastair Roberts, "The Politics of the King's Donkey," *Political Theology.com*, http://www.politicaltheology.com/blog/the-politics-of-the-kings-donkey-luke-1928-40/ (accessed September 27, 2016).

THE DISTRIBUTION OF CHRIST'S SPIRIT

A further passage that can help us to unlock the riches of
Acts 2 is found in Numbers 11. In that chapter, Moses
appealed to the Lord to reduce the burden of leadership
that was upon his shoulders. In an event redolent of the
Sinai theophany in some key details, God took of the Spirit
that was upon Moses and put it on the seventy elders.[5]
This donation of the Spirit to the elders was mediated by
Moses: the gift of the Spirit was a "membering" of, or ap-
portioning of shares within, Moses' own gift. The elders
do not receive the Spirit in the form of an immediate be-
stowal of God, but as a participation in Moses' ministry.
Thereafter they can represent Moses to the people without
displacing him. When the Spirit descends upon the elders,
they prophesy as a sign of their new gift, a phenomenon
that will not be repeated again (11:25).

Within this passage Moses declares his wish that "all
the Lord's people were prophets and that the Lord would
put His Spirit upon them" (11:29).[6] This desire is later re-
articulated in the form of promise in Joel 2:28-29:

> And it shall come to pass afterward
> That I will pour out My Spirit on all flesh;
> Your sons and your daughters shall prophesy,
> Your old men shall dream dreams,
> Your young men shall see visions;

---

[5] For the parallels with Sinai, note that both events involve: (1) the
granting of a new vocation to a group of people (Ex. 19:5-6; Num.
11:16-17); (2) a command for them to sanctify themselves in preparation for the coming day when the LORD will act (Ex. 19:10; Num.
11:18); (3) the assembling of the people around a particular location—
Mount Sinai in Exodus and the tent of meeting in Numbers; (4) a theophany event where God descends in a cloud to speak with Moses.

[6] All references to Scripture are to the New King James Version.

> And also on My menservants and on My
> maidservants
> I will pour out My Spirit in those days.

It is this passage that Peter references in his Pentecost sermon, declaring that the events of that day are in fulfilment of Joel's prophecy (Acts 2:16-21). Lurking behind Joel's prophecy is Numbers 11 and the membering of the Spirit upon Moses to the seventy elders. At Pentecost, the promise of the Spirit received by Christ from the Father (2:33) is "membered," given to the disciples, who now bear his authority and act in his name and as his representatives.

THE RUDIMENTS OF AN ECCLESIOLOGY

Within the discussion above, the rudiments of an ecclesiology have started to emerge. The Church is a body of people formed of many different nations and language groups. It is a fulfilment of the promised blessing of Abraham, as people formerly divided and alienated from God by judgment are brought together in a single body.

It is a people constituted by the gift of the Spirit, who writes the Law of God on our hearts and sets us apart for ministry. The Church is a new temple, a habitation for God in the Spirit. The gift of the Spirit—understood against the background of the theophany of Exodus 19 and 20—is fundamentally the inscription of the Word upon us and the empowering and authorizing of us by the Word placed within us. This gift is manifested in the powerful preaching of the gospel to all.

The ministry and authority of the Church flows from the ministry and authority of Christ. As Christ gives us his Spirit, the Church's ministry is conformed to Christ's own ministry, exhibiting a similar shape. However, the Spirit is never detached from Christ, nor does the Church ever replace Christ. Rather, we receive the Spirit as a membering of Christ's own Spirit. We act in his name, are empowered by his strength, participate in his sonship, and labor as those completing his mission. Christ continues his mission through us.

Pentecost displays the truth at the heart of Reformed ecclesiology: the Church is a body formed by the power of the Word and manifested in the preaching of that Word. The Church finds the sole source of its identity and spiritual power in its dependence upon its head, Jesus Christ, whose place no other can usurp. The Spirit that we receive is a membering of his Spirit: the flames upon us are always already divided, their tongues only united in their source. The gift of the unmembered Spirit without measure is only the possession of the Church in the person of its head and he is the only one who ever mediates its gift.

LESSONS FROM THE AFTERSHOCKS

Following the earthquake that was the Day of Pentecost, there is a small succession of "aftershock" events, as the Spirit is received by a number of other parties or as the disciples experience a renewed encounter with the Spirit's power (Acts 4:31; 8:14-17; 10:44-45; 11:15; 19:1-6). These events present us with a more complicated picture, while bringing certain dynamics into clearer expression. They help us address the question I raised at the outset concerning the downstream movement of the Spirit in relation to the Church.

The first key event occurred as the Samaritans responded in faith to the preaching of Philip in Acts 8:4-8 and were baptized. The Jerusalem apostles sent Peter and John to them, who prayed that the Samaritans should receive the Holy Spirit. After laying hands on them, the Spirit came upon the Samaritans. The second event occurred as Peter declared the gospel to Cornelius' house and, while he was still speaking, the Spirit fell upon those hearing his word (10:44; 11:15). The third event involved about twelve disciples of John the Baptist who had only been baptized by John's baptism. After Paul instructed them concerning the meaning of John's baptism and declared the gospel to them, they were baptized in Jesus' name. Then Paul laid hands on them and they spoke with tongues and prophesied.

A striking feature of these accounts is the contrasting order within them. In the case of the Samaritans, the order of events is (1) hearing the gospel, (2) faith, (3) baptism, (4) apostles' prayer for them to receive the Spirit, (5) laying on of the apostles' hands, (6) reception of the Spirit. In the case of Cornelius and his household there is (1) an anticipatory form of faith, (2) hearing of the gospel, (3) Christian faith, (4) reception of the Spirit, and then (5) baptism. Finally, in the case of the Ephesian disciples of John, there is (1) an anticipatory form of faith, (2) hearing of the gospel, (3) Christian faith, (4) baptism, (5) laying on of hands, and (6) reception of the Spirit.

Through the disruptions and inconsistencies of the patterns, in addition to certain elements within the sequences, the divine prerogative in giving the Spirit is emphasized. The occurrence of prayer preceding the apostles' laying on of their hands upon the Samaritans makes clear that it wasn't an autonomous power they possessed (as Simon the sorcerer seems to have supposed—8:14-25).

The unexpected descent of the Spirit upon Cornelius and his household, before Peter had baptized or laid hands on them, served as a divine testimony to God's welcome of the Gentiles: Peter's performance of baptism was purely responsive in this situation. The gift of the Spirit is not tied to the action of the Church and its ministers, but can occur independent of it.

Yet there are congruencies, which highlight the fact that God ordinarily works through the ministration of the Church. Especially in the case of the gift of the Spirit to the Samaritans we see God acting in a way that establishes the importance of the apostles within his Church. The structure and institution is thus upheld by the manner of divine action, but it remains clear that God can and does act beyond and apart from this. The pouring out of the Spirit on Cornelius' household illustrates this. Once again, the fact that Peter, the pre-eminent apostle, is divinely chosen to pioneer the ministry to the Gentiles reinforces the institution of the Church, yet the fact that God pours out the Spirit apart from Peter's laying on of hands makes clear that, while the Church and its ministers may ordinarily be the means of God's action, he is by no means tied to them.

An illustrative parallel to this can be found in a dimension of the account of Numbers 11. The seventy elders are assembled around the tabernacle and the Spirit of Moses is placed upon them. However, two of the elders, Eldad and Medad, had remained in the camp, and yet the Spirit came upon them too, causing them to prophesy in the midst of the camp (Numbers 11:26-30). Upon hearing a report of this, Joshua called Moses to forbid them, but Moses refused to do so, questioning whether Joshua was jealous for his sake and expressing his desire that all of God's people would prophesy.

This event is strongly reminiscent of the gospel account of Luke 9:49-50, where John declared that they had forbidden someone from casting out demons in Jesus' name, because he wasn't a member of the apostolic band. Jesus responds much like Moses, charging his disciples not to forbid such a person "for he who is not against us is for us." Both Moses and Jesus resist attempts to restrict the Spirit's ministry and prerogative to the ordered institution, which, although it is the ordinary form of the Spirit's action, is not the only form. Eldad and Medad may not have been among the elders around the tabernacle and the exorcist of Luke 9:49 may not have been a member of the apostolic band, but each of these people has a part in the ministry and the Spirit. The Church exceeds the institution. Like Joshua, there is no need for us to be jealous on Christ's account, for all with the Spirit, whether or not they are within the institution, are members of him.

Within the book of Acts, we find a number of encounters with believing persons and teachers outside of the official apostolic group. Faced with people who manifested the work and gifting of the Spirit, the Church's task was one of recognition of and celebration of God's work. Characters such as Ananias (Acts 9:10-19), Barnabas (9:26-27), Peter (11:27), and Aquila and Priscilla (18:24-28) are all set forth in the book of Acts as persons prepared to welcome and support the work of God in unexpected and seemingly unauthorized places and persons. Aquila and Priscilla's reception and support of the ministry of Apollos is exemplary here, illustrating the way in which more "official" ministers of the church could practice a posture of openness to God's ministers beyond the official channels of the institutional church.

How then should we understand baptism, which seems to be naturally connected with the ministry and membership of the institutional church? Within Acts there is an intimate connection between faith, reception of the Spirit, belonging to the Church, and baptism, something apparent in places such as Acts 2:38. Baptism, then, does not seem to be at the root of what is required for inclusion in Christ. Must we then evacuate it of any meaning, reducing it to an empty sign?

The answer, I believe, is found in the Reformed tradition's recognition of baptism as a promissory and confirmatory seal. Baptism is a divinely instituted rite, by which we are marked out by a promise.[7] This rite publicly confirms our standing to us and to others in a manner that strengthens faith. It is a means by which we are granted to receive and grasp onto the reality that it signifies. The relationship between baptism and membership of Christ is akin to the relationship between accession to the throne and coronation: the two are intimately and inseparably connected in the ordinary manner of things, yet it is possible for one to occur without the other. The ruling status of the monarch is not directly dependent upon their coronation, but the coronation confirms and publicly manifests that status. Likewise, baptism is the ordinary means of our reception into the Church, yet is not the basis or cause of our membership, nor so necessarily tied to it that we could not be members of the visible Church apart from it.

---

[7] See my discussion of this in Alastair Roberts, "Infant Baptism and the Promise of Grace," *Reformation21.org*, http://www.reformation21.org/articles/infant-baptism-and-the-when-of-baptismal-grace.php (accessed September 27, 2016).

Baptism is also a sign to the church itself. It is the continual practice of our recognition and reception of the work of God, our posture of openness to the Lord who is adding to us. In baptizing someone we are recognizing and declaring their membership in Christ, rather than creating it. In each baptism, we perform the fundamental Christian act of welcoming our brothers and sisters (Romans 15:7), expressing the same submissive posture before the act of God as that expressed by the Apostle Peter in Acts 11:17: "If therefore God gave them the same gift as He gave us when we believed on the Lord Jesus Christ, who was I that I could withstand God?"

CONCLUSION

Within Luke's accounts of Pentecost and its aftermath there is a rich ecclesiological vision that both resonates with and fills out the more explicit ecclesiology found within the epistles. Beyond bolstering and consolidating the ecclesiology that we might have developed from the epistles, the narrative of Acts firmly grounds the ecclesiology of the New Testament more generally in God's climactic work within history. It reveals that the ecclesiology of the New Testament is not the child of abstract theologizing, but the product of close and receptive reflection upon concrete divine acts, from which the doctrine could be derived.

What Acts further discloses is something of the genealogy of New Testament ecclesiology. The event of Pentecost only makes its true sense when understood within a scriptural matrix, as it is related to what went before. In the Church of Pentecost we find new conjugations of old roots, roots that are shared with Old Testament realities and events. Pentecost is in continuity with these, while also being a radical escalation of God's work in history.

The events of Pentecost come at the fulfilment and culmination of a long history that precedes them. With the sound from heaven as of a rushing mighty wind, the Church is set aflame by the power of the Word of God and equipped to declare this Word to all of the nations. The countless expectant whispers of an Old Testament choir of witnesses, their disparate voices drawn from throughout the canon, now combine and swell by the Spirit into a glorious and triumphant declaration of the fulfilment of divine pledge and purpose. Against the backdrop of this history we see more clearly who we are as God's people, and are driven on a wave of redoubled promise towards the future furnished for us.

PART III:
PROTESTANT ECCLESIOLOGY IN HISTORY

VI:

SIMUL JUSTUS ET PECCATOR: THE GENIUS AND TENSIONS OF REFORMATION ECCLESIOLOGY

Bradford Littlejohn

THE GENIUS OF LUTHER'S ECCLESIOLOGY

IT IS often remarked that Martin Luther did not set out to make a new church, just to reform the old one. This is true enough, but if it is meant to imply (as it sometimes is) that Luther was not up to anything terribly radical, that the Reformation was just a big misunderstanding, then it is gravely misleading. For Luther did mean to offer a new understanding of *what the church was*—not wholly new, of course, but radically new from the standpoint of the later Middle Ages. He writes in his *Letter to the Christian Nobility of the German Nation*:

> all Christians are truly of the spiritual estate, and there is no difference among them except that of office. Paul says in 1 Corinthians 12 that we are all one body, yet every member has its own work by which it serves the others. This is because we have one baptism, one Gospel, one faith, and are all Christians alike;

> for baptism, Gospel, and faith make us spir-
> itual and a Christian people.[1]

The church, in short, is all of us, everyone who calls on the name of the Lord. Indeed, so far from the clergy constituting the church, the church constitutes the clergy. This was a profound shift from the irreducibly institutional understanding of the church in medieval Catholicism, for which "the Church" meant above all an authority structure, with the Pope squarely at its head.

From one standpoint, Luther's redefinition appeared to offer a straightforward and empirical account of what the church was: an assembly of people—or rather, the whole sum of assemblies throughout the world of people—who call on the name of Christ. But properly speaking, this was not so much an account of what the church *was* but of where you found it. The Church itself, wrote Luther, "is a high, deep, hidden thing which one may neither perceive nor see but must grasp only by faith through baptism, sacrament, and word."[2] It was not so much an empirical assembly of bodies as "a spiritual assembly of souls in one faith . . . The natural, real, and essential Christendom exists in the Spirit and not in any external thing."[3] After all, if the Church was nothing but the body of Christ, and none could be united to Christ except by faith, and

---

[1] In *Three Treatises, from the American Edition of Luther's Works* (Minneapolis: Fortress Press, 1966), 12.

[2] *D. Martin Luther's Werke: kritische Gesamtausgabe (Weimarer Ausgabe)*, 120 vols, (Weimar: H. Böhlaus Nachfolger, 1883–2009), 51:507, quoted in Paul D.L. Avis, *The Church in the Theology of the Reformers* (London: Marshall, Morgan, and Scott, 1981), 14.

[3] *Luther's Works: American Edition*, edited by Jaroslav Pelikan and Helmut T. Lehmann (St. Louis: Concordia Publishing House, and Philadelphia: Muhlenberg Press, 1955–1970), 39:69, quoted in Avis, 14.

faith was itself a "high, deep, hidden thing," then how could the true Church not be likewise?

But lest this notion of the Church suggest something static and abstract, a mere logical sum of individual believers, we should note that Luther describes the Church in far more dynamic terms than that. The Church is the creature of the living and active Word of God, and particularly the Word as preached. "The Church is nothing without the word and everything in it exists by virtue of the word alone."[4] Indeed, "The Church of God is present wherever the word of God is spoken, whether it be in the middle of the Turks' land or in the pope's land or in hell itself. For it is the word of God which builds the Church which is lord over all other spaces."[5]

The Church, thus, is in itself invisible, but it becomes visible when that which gives it life, the Word, is preached, heard, acknowledged, and obeyed in the world. We may, however—indeed must for practical purposes—speak of the regular organized assembly of professing believers who worship in word and sacrament as the "visible church," with appropriate caveats. Luther's concept of the justified sinner, *simul justus et peccator*, sometimes provided him a framework for ecclesiology. The church was at the same time perfectly righteous by virtue of its union with Christ, but this union, and this righteous identity, were hidden; as manifest in the world, in history, it was still sinful and failing, a *corpus permixtum* composed of wheat and tares, gradually being sanctified. And yet there remained certain "notes" or "marks" by which the true church could be visibly recognized in history. The Augsburg Confession of

---

[4] *Luther's Works*, 40:11, quoted in Avis, 20.

[5] *Weimarer Ausgabe*, 43.596, quoted in Avis, 20.

1530 established two marks: "The Church is the congregation of saints, in which the Gospel is rightly taught and the Sacraments are rightly administered."[6] But some over the next couple decades sought to emphasize that just as true Christians must be characterized by godly life, so must the true church. Accordingly, they added a third mark, "discipline," which initially had quite a broad sense, rather than simply designating excommunication and its precursors.[7]

THE TENSIONS OF LUTHER'S ECCLESIOLOGY

Such marks were all fairly useful in giving you a decent idea of roughly where the church *was* (although they obviously could not stand alone; they presupposed a Protestant understanding of what the Gospel and sacraments were): if you saw a minister faithfully expounding the text of Scripture, and administering baptism and the Lord's Supper, well then you could assume that there was a manifestation of Christ's body; imperfect, perhaps, but in communion with the Head. But they weren't so good at telling you where the church *wasn't*.[8] How false did a church's preach-

---

6 Art. VII (http://bookofconcord.org/augsburgconfession.php [accessed May 27, 2014]).

7 See Jordan J. Ballor and W. Bradford Littlejohn, "European Calvinism: Church Discipline," in Irene Dingel and Johannes Paulmann, eds., *European History Online* (EGO) (Mainz: Institute of European History (IEG), 2013): http://www.ieg-ego.eu/en/threads/crossroads/religious-and-denominational-spaces/jordan-ballor-w-bradford-littlejohn-european-calvinism-church-discipline.

8 Paul D.L. Avis, "The True Church in Reformation Theology," *Scottish Journal of Theology* 30, no. 4 (1977): 334: "The *notae ecclesiae* is a qualitative concept; theoretically one can say whether a certain ecclesial body possesses the marks or not. But in practice it was found to need supplementing by a quantitative one, such as Calvin's concept that Rome contained the *vestigia* of the church."

ing have to be before it could no longer count as part of the body of Christ? How distorted or rationalistic or superstitious did its sacramental practice have to be? How lax did its discipline have to be?

Luther's theology offered no clear answers to such questions. It also opened itself to other dangers. The clarion call of the *Letter to the Christian Nobility* was, after all, a double-edged sword. So long as the Church was dominated by corrupt clergy, it made good sense to remind the Christian laity that they too were called to be kings and priests to God. They too had responsibility for the welfare of the Church, and they must do all in their power to see it reformed—especially those whom God had placed in positions of authority. But what about once a faithful ministry of godly clergy had been established? Should lay rulers continue to exercise control over the affairs of the Church?

Luther and his colleague Melanchthon hesitated, but ultimately acknowledged a substantial ongoing role for civil magistrates in church affairs. Indeed, it was their very emphasis on the hiddenness of the true church that determined this conclusion: since we must be very wary of trying to draw precise boundaries around the truly faithful Christians, we must accept for practical purposes that all those who professed Christianity belonged to the Church, and this meant nearly the whole body of citizens. In its temporal profile, then, the Church overlapped almost wholly with the body politic, and hence decisions about its temporal well-being were fit subjects for the civil magistrate's concern.[9] The same basic assumption, with slight

---

[9] For the best treatment of Luther and Melanchthon's understanding of the role of magistracy in the church, see James M. Estes, *Peace, Order,*

differences of emphasis, was to inform Zwingli's reform in Zurich, Bucer's reform in Strasbourg, and the various phases of the English Reformation.

Still, while coherent enough in principle, the new Protestant ecclesiology was shot through with tensions in practice, and a range of rival models for resolving these tensions soon emerged.

ATTEMPTED SOLUTIONS TO THE TENSIONS OF PROTESTANT ECCLESIOLOGY

The Anabaptist Model

The first, one with which Luther himself had briefly sympathized, but which was before long rejected by all the leading Reformers, was the Anabaptist option. Although there were several independent and rather different strands of the Anabaptist movement, the most important was probably that which arose in Zurich and its environs under the leadership of Conrad Grebel and Balthasar Hubmaier in the mid-1520s. Zurich had embraced a particularly thoroughgoing model of the partnership between magistracy and ministry, and although the Reformation there was real and resulted in the conversion of many, Grebel and Hubmaier were appalled by the slow pace of reform and the nominalism of so much of the populace. The Church in Zurich was self-evidently not identical with the city's whole population, and leaders like Grebel and Hubmaier did not think that such an ambiguous state of affairs should be tolerated. Anabaptism is best known for its insistence on re-baptism and its critique of civil authority,

---

and the Glory of God: Secular Authority and the Church in the Thought of Luther and Melanchthon, 1518–1559 (Leiden: Brill, 2005).

but both of these positions must be understood against the larger background of the Anabaptist aim to establish a visible congregation of saints that truly was the Church and nothing but the Church. Writes Kenneth Davis,

> Contrary to most Magisterial reformers' exegesis, most Anabaptists upheld that while society at large could correspond to the parable of the tares (Matt. 13) and openly include believers and unbelievers, the church could not. Rather, each church, as a corporate entity, was to be visibly and voluntarily (without any civil constraints) holy, an approximation of the heavenly, spiritual kingdom on earthly collective display.[10]

This entailed not only limiting church membership to those who voluntarily committed themselves by baptism, but also carefully policing church membership by rigorous discipline ("the ban") to remove false Christians from the fellowship. Despite the complexity and variety of the Anabaptist movements, this emphasis on discipline was a consistent theme.

The Strasbourg Model

It was also a theme that found a sympathetic hearing among several of the Reformers, including Martin Bucer at Strasbourg and his protégé, John Calvin. Of course, the word "discipline" could mean many different things. Although the word easily carries a negative connotation, for Bucer, it primarily meant something like "corporate sancti-

---

[10] Kenneth R. Davis, "No Discipline, No Church: An Anabaptist Contribution to the Reformed Tradition," *The Sixteenth Century Journal* 13, no. 4 (1982): 44.

fication." "Discipline" meant a Christian community's determination to live out Christian love toward one another.[11] Of course, this did not happen spontaneously. It required structures, rules, and where necessary, *discipline* in the more precise sense of corrective imposition of these rules. As an outward action, discipline in this sense could never guarantee inward renewal (hence there was, for Bucer and Calvin, no question of the Anabaptist notion that the visible church might be brought to match the invisible), but the Strasbourg reformer believed that if administered rightly by ministers, church discipline could have a much better chance of prompting real repentance than the merely civil discipline practiced at Zwingli and Bullinger's Zurich (where even excommunication functioned as a civil penalty prescribed by magistrates).

Bucer's interest in a church discipline which could at least reduce the gap between the church visible and invisible proved broadly appealing and inspiring for other reformers, with at least two different models emerging. One, associated with John Calvin, proved best suited to city-states or small polities with relatively sympathetic magistrates. It had considerably less in common with modern Presbyterianism than we generally imagine: Calvin's "deacons" were civil officers charged with overseeing welfare distributions, and the "elders" functioned not merely alongside the ministers on the Consistory, but as leading city councilors of Geneva. Magistrates even had an im-

---

[11] See Jake Meador, "'That No One Should Live for Himself, but for Others': Love and the Third Mark of the Church in the Theology of Martin Bucer," in W. Bradford Littlejohn and Jonathan Tomes, ed., *Beyond Calvin: Essays on the Diversity of the Reformed Tradition* (Moscow, ID: The Davenant Press, 2017).

portant role in matters of worship and church order.[12] Indeed, Calvin accepted no less than did the Zurich reformers a Christendom model, in which the church of Geneva and the citizenry of Geneva made up one and the same society. However, there were some points of ambiguity and tension. First was the role of the ministers, who for Calvin had a direct divine calling as well as a human ordination. While not denying Luther's notion of the universal priesthood, Calvin did put more emphasis on the distinctiveness of the clerical calling, and wanted to avoid any implication that ministers might be mere officers of state (though he did allow to magistrates an important role in confirming their appointment).[13] Second was the power of excommunication, which for Calvin was a spiritual exercise of discipline necessary to guard the purity of the Lord's Table, not a mere civil penalty for wicked behavior, and as such, wholly under the authority of ministers and of the elders *acting in their ecclesiastical capacity* as members of the Consistory. Given the dual role of most of Geneva's elders, it is easy to see why the City Council struggled to see the importance of the neat distinction, but for Calvin, it was essential.[14]

As a contribution to Protestant ecclesiology, Calvin's institutionalization of church discipline at Geneva was both blessing and curse. At its best, it testified to the essential Protestant insight that the only authority in the

---

[12] Matthew Tuininga, *Calvin's Political Theology and the Public Engagement of the Church: Christ's Two Kingdoms* (Cambridge: CUP, 2017), chs. 5, 8.

[13] *Institutes of the Christian Religion* IV.4.13.

[14] For a good survey, see Gillian Lewis, "Calvinism in Geneva in the Time of Calvin and Beza (1541–1605)," in Menna Prestwich, ed., *International Calvinism, 1541–1715* (Oxford: Clarendon Press, 1985), 39-70.

Church was the authority of the Word: only the internally convicting power of the Word, not any external punishments, was the means to bring repentance and restoration to the Christian and to build up the community of the Church. But it was easy for the emphasis to be displaced from the minister's *declaration* to the minister's *office*. This effectively erected another parallel juridical authority within the Christian society with the capacity to administer what amounted—in such a society—to a civil as well as spiritual punishment, and often with much greater strictness than any civil court would. The Consistory at Geneva, and its many imitators elsewhere, were certainly not always that bad; but the system was certainly ripe for abuses.

It is important to note, however, that despite his fame, John Calvin was perhaps not the most important contributor to Reformed ecclesiology. After all, Calvin's model of the church assumed close cooperation between magistracy and ministry, and thus required not only a sympathetic magistrate, but a relatively small or decentralized polity. It thus proved influential in the Swiss city-states and in the quasi-autonomous cities of the Netherlands, and was even adopted (though with profound tensions) in the small kingdom of Scotland, but it required extensive adaptation in other settings.

A better model for a more-or-less autonomous church in the midst of an unfriendly society was pioneered by the Polish Reformer Jan Łaski, who spent most of his ministry in the Netherlands and England. Like Bucer, with whom had worked closely, he felt the need to respond to Anabaptist pressures, and during his tenure as superintendent of the church at Emden (1542-48) adopted a stricter discipline administered by lay-elders within the congregation. But he first had a free hand to develop his ideas fully as pastor of the London Strangers' Church, a collection of congregations composed of Dutch and French Protestant refugees which Łaski administered from 1548 to 1553. There Łaski, together with French pastor Valérand Poullain (1509?-1557), pioneered the creation of a form of church discipline (described in his *Forma ac ratio*) that, although retaining the emphasis on discipline as a means of edification, and redemption of recalcitrant sinners, was particularly severe even by the standards of the day.[15] Moreover, since the English authorities gave the exiles freedom to govern their own affairs quasi-autonomously, Łaski was able to create a church structure remarkably reminiscent of the Anabaptist ideal—a gathered, self-governing community of believers who agreed to commit themselves to the biblically-modeled system of discipline, which helped purify the body of the faithful from the "tares" of worldly Christians.[16]

---

[15] As Michael Springer relates in *Restoring Christ's Church: John á Lasco and the Forma Ac Ratio* (Aldershot: Ashgate, 2007), one striking example of Łaski's disciplinary zeal was his directive in the *Forma ac ratio* for ministers to visit anyone who fell ill in their congregation, in order to "warn the afflicted that God uses illness as a warning and evidence of his divine justice, and that the stricken should endure it with patience and gratitude…. [And] because the illness had been sent as a punishment, the preacher or elder should encourage the parishioner to reconcile with anyone they had offended" (92).

[16] Particularly remarkable in this regard was the insistence in the *Forma ac ratio* that the sacraments could be only be administered to individuals who had pledged to abide fully by the discipline of the community. See Springer, *Restoring Christ's Church*, 84, 87. If we define the Anabaptist or "radical" ecclesiology according to the four themes identified by Paul Avis in his *Church in the Theology of the Reformers* (pp. 55-61)—voluntarism, primitivism, exclusivism, and obsession with discipline—it is hard not to see the influence of this model on Łaski's ecclesiology. A distinctive element in Łaski's system, however, which certainly ran contrary to

By its very presence at the heart of London, Łaski's church exerted a radicalizing influence on many in England, and perhaps even on the Scottish reformer John Knox (c. 1514-1572), who was preaching in London at this time.[17] When Mary I (1516-1558) took the throne in 1553, the members of the Stranger churches, their ranks swelled by fleeing English Protestants, scattered to several continental havens, bringing the model of Łaski's *Forma ac ratio* with them—back to Emden, to Frankfurt, and even to Geneva. Łaski scholar Michael Springer has compellingly argued that the English exile churches in Frankfurt and even Geneva itself (which John Knox pastored) modeled themselves chiefly after Łaski's Strangers' Church, and not, as usually assumed, after Calvin's Geneva.[18] The influence of Łaski's model was also to be felt in the Netherlands and in the French Reformed Church, which although deeply influenced by Calvin and Beza at Geneva, had to adapt their model for use in a setting where churches could not rely on the support of magistrates.

Łaski's model, more than any, seems to lend itself to the use of a disestablished Protestant church, such as those in America and indeed in most of the world today. However, by its zeal to identify and police the boundaries of that church, it runs the sectarian risk of Anabaptism, and of trying to erase too much the gap between the visible

---

Anabaptist congregationalism, was the office of superintendent, a quasi-bishop or permanent moderator of sorts for a small group of congregations, who helped oversee their administration and guide their teaching. Unlike Lutheran superintendents or English bishops, however, Łaski's superintendents were chosen by congregants, not magistrates. See Springer, *Restoring Christ's Church*, 62-67.

[17] See Springer, *Restoring Christ's Church*, 86-89.

[18] See Springer, *Restoring Christ's Church*, 126-32.

and invisible churches. This danger was to become particularly clear in Elizabethan Puritanism, which seems to have drawn as much inspiration from the London Strangers' Church as it did from Geneva. But to understand this movement, we must briefly touch on one other model for Protestant church-polity.

The Nation-State Model

If Bullinger, Bucer, and Calvin had all sketched ways of organizing a church within a small polity governed by sympathetic magistrates, and Łaski had provided a model that could work without the support of any magistrates, what about a Protestant church in a very large polity, and a monarchical one at that, like England? Here the centralization of authority in the monarch and the basically hierarchical structure of society worked against any notion of a democratic, bottom-up church. A totally independent church hierarchy deriving its authority from Christ above, on the other hand, would have perpetuated the intolerable church-state conflicts of the late Middle Ages, and tended to reinscribe the clericalism that Luther had fought so hard to overcome.

Accordingly, the most natural solution was to maintain two distinct hierarchies, the bishops and the nobility, which joined at the top—working together in Parliament, under the sole sovereignty of the monarch. Of course, after the early hubris of King Henry VIII, there was no question of the monarch actually exercising or being the source of spiritual authority—the bishops and the presbyters exercised their spiritual calling of Word and Sacrament on behalf of Christ, but their particular appointments, and their position in the hierarchy, were determined by human authority, with the monarch as its focal point. And Luther's principle of the universal priesthood was operative enough in England for most of its bishops to recognize that laymen in Parliament, and the monarch as the *praecipuum membrum ecclesia* ("foremost member of the church," a phrase of Melanchthon's), had a legitimate role in making decisions about what Scripture and prudence required for matters of church order.[19]

The fact that a rather similar episcopal structure prevailed in Lutheran Denmark and Sweden suggests that the distinctive shape of the Church of England is less the result of a particular "genius of Anglicanism," and more the natural fruit of Protestant ecclesiology adapting itself to a monarchical nation-state. Of course, the adaptation was not without profound tensions, any more than the other models we have seen. In England, at least, three distinct sources of tension may be noted.

The first concerned the relation of Crown and Parliament, and the distinct elements of Parliament to one another. In particular, did the bishops report directly to the monarch, or did the laymen in Parliament also have a role in overseeing them—or did the bishops together with the lay Lords and Commons make up Parliament together, and relate to the monarch in that capacity?

The second concerned the difficulty, within such a large hierarchical church structure, of bishops being sufficiently responsive to the bottom and top simultaneously— to the practical on-the-ground needs of pastors and churchgoers, and to the wishes and demands of the mon-

---

[19] For a still-excellent treatment of the understanding of monarch and bishops in the early Church of England, see Norman Sykes, *Old Priest and New Presbyter* (Cambridge: CUP, 1957).

arch and of national political realities. Some bishops were indeed worldly time-servers, as many of their critics charged, but most were earnest and godly men torn between numerous often-conflicting obligations.[20]

The third concerned the same basic tension that bedeviled Protestant ecclesiology from the beginning: how to live with the obvious disconnect between a body calling itself "the Church," the bride of Christ, and a Church made up of men and women who, for the most part, seemed to understand little of the faith they professed on Sundays and to practice even less of it on weekdays.

The first of these issues, being largely one of political theory, will not detain us here, but the latter two proved to be generative of more than a century of profound conflict within the Protestant Church of England, and bequeathed to us in America (our forefathers often refugees from these conflicts) much of our distinctive approach to ecclesiology.

THE PURITAN MOVEMENT

The Puritan movement was birthed out of profound dissatisfaction with how the bishops had handled the so-called Second Vestiarian Controversy in the 1560s. In her restoration of Protestant worship to England in 1559, Elizabeth had taken a relatively conservative line to ease the transition for those of her subjects less than thrilled about the new state of affairs. In particular, she required clergy to wear many of the same vestments that their

---

[20] For a sympathetic portrait, see Patrick Collinson, *The Religion of Protestants: The Church in English Society, 1559–1625* (Oxford: Clarendon Press, 1982), and Kenneth Fincham, *Prelate as Pastor: The Episcopate of James I* (Oxford: Clarendon Press, 1990).

Catholic predecessors had, while leading worship. Many ministers felt that, rather than making it easier for them to win more Catholic-minded parishioners, these vestments simply offended the sensibilities of the godly, who could not overcome their popish associations. Many of the bishops sympathized with this concern, but when the Queen proved emphatic, they reasoned that discretion was the better part of valor and enforced conformity, deeming that there was nothing intrinsically ungodly about the vestments.

Feeling betrayed, many young leaders in the church began to question the authority of bishops altogether, as well as the multitude of outward ceremonies and orders in the Church of England that were retained from its pre-Reformation days. Indeed, by appealing to the senses rather than the soul, these outward ornaments helped lull the nominal Christians (who made up the vast majority in England, they charged) into complacency. While for the most part not rejecting the notion of a comprehensive national church, the emerging Puritan party somehow hoped to purify it by learned preaching, stripped-down ceremonies, and rigorous discipline so that it consisted as much as possible only of those who were truly godly. For many of them, a key part of this process was abolishing bishops and replacing them with a presbyterian or quasi-congregational system in which pastors and elders oversaw a largely autonomous church structure.[21]

Such autonomy either implied a parallel hierarchy and jurisdiction alongside the civil one, which seemed a recipe

---

[21] The classic treatment, even if it needs updating in various details, remains Patrick Collinson, *The Elizabethan Puritan Movement* (Oxford: Clarendon, 1967).

for civil war, or else a separatist sect dedicated to maintaining a pure fellowship of the godly within its bounds, while the majority of the national church was consigned to perdition.[22] Although Elizabethan authorities understandably feared the former most of all, seeing it as a new popery, it was not until the 1640s that these fears came to partial fruition, and that was the perhaps predictable result of episcopal tyranny in the 1630s. The latter threat, however, that of separatism, was to gain traction in the 1590s and early 1600s, eventually spawning many of the first immigrants to America.

Of course, from our standpoint we would be quick to point out that there is nothing intrinsically wrong with a disestablished, self-governing church; such was the Church before Constantine and such are all our churches in America today. However, problems do arise when such a church organizes itself within a broader society and church which considers itself genuinely Christian. In such a setting, it is easy for the separating church to think that the reason for its separation is that the broader church *isn't really Christian after all*, and then to suppose that it, the separated church, *really is*. Sometimes, the separating church is right about this; but this move can represent an attempt to carve out a visible church made up only of members of the invisible church, rather than accepting that the church that we see is a mixed multitude of saints and sinners, and its structures more human than divine. Having made this move intellectually, the separated church then tries to reinforce it culturally by fostering an implacable opposition to and with-

---

[22] For a good survey, see Stephen Brachlow, *The Communion of Saints: Radical Puritan and Separatist Ecclesiology, 1570–1625* (Oxford: Oxford University Press, 1988).

drawal from the culture and practices of the broader society.

All of this characterized the separatist wing of the Puritan movement in the Church of England, and because they brought with them to the New World this need to define themselves against a nominal broader church, the Puritans in New England soon found themselves squabbling over purity, drawing boundaries, and separating from one another in a process that was to play out interminably in the centuries that followed.[23]

CONCLUSION

The genius of Protestant ecclesiology is same as that of Protestant soteriology—as the individual lives by faith alone, so does the Church. The Christian cannot seek his identity in anything that he brings or does, but only by throwing himself on Christ by faith in the Word proclaimed, and trusting that his life is hidden with Christ in God. Likewise, the Christian Church cannot seek its identity in its outward form or practices, but only by receiving its being from Christ by the Word proclaimed in its midst, and trusting that its true life too is hidden with Christ in God.

But the tension and struggle of Protestant ecclesiology is the same as that of Protestant soteriology—how is faith attested, manifested, and recognized by its works of obedience? How does the unseen church of faith make

---

[23] The early New England phases of this divisiveness are well chronicled in Michael P. Winship, *Godly Republicanism: Puritans, Pilgrims, and a City on a Hill* (Cambridge, MA: Harvard University Press, 2012); the later 19th-century phases in John Williamson Nevin, "The Sect System, Article 1," *Mercersburg Review* 1, no. 5 (1849): 482-507.

itself visible by rendering corporate obedience to Christ, governing and ordering itself in accordance with his Word and the demands of discipleship? If Luther was sometimes too content to leave the sanctification of the church in merely human hands, the Anabaptists, and occasionally some of the Reformed, were too quick to seek for the Spirit's fingerprints in the outward life of the body. The same polarity appeared in the conflicts of the Church of England, and it continues today, for instance in the battle between evangelical megachurches that ask only a minimalist profession of faith and stern Reformed churches that impose strict discipline on their faithful few.

It is a tension that defies any conclusive, once-for-all resolution, but the approach of English theologian Richard Hooker in the 1590s may still offer us some valuable light. "Signs must resemble the things they signify," he declares, and we might legitimately speak of the visible church, in his theology, as a sign which signifies the presence of the invisible. Accordingly, it must strive to manifest outwardly the qualities which it has antecedently in Christ:

> That which inwardly each man should be, the Church outwardly ought to testify. And therefore the duties of our religion which are seen must be such as that affection which is unseen ought to be. Signs must resemble the things they signify. If religion bear the greatest sway in our hearts, our outward religious duties must show it, as far as the Church hath outward ability. . . . Yea then are the public duties of religion best ordered, when the militant Church doth resemble by sensible means, as it may in such cases, the hidden dignity and glo-

ry wherewith the Church triumphant in heav-
en is beautified.[24]

This hidden glory includes both unity and purity. But
like all outward manifestations, such unity and purity are to
be treated under the heading of the doctrine of sanctification. But just because sanctification must be distinguished
from justification does not mean it should be separated:
the sanctification of the church is the process of it becoming more conformed to its hidden reality, righteous in
Christ. Hooker, accordingly, is well-prepared to argue at
length for the importance of historical structures of authority, visible forms of unity, liturgical aids to holiness,
diligent observance of the sacraments, and submission to
creedal and confessional norms as the signs and seals of
the church's hidden life, crucial to its sanctification and
well-being.[25] But these things do not constitute the
church's being, the basis of its recognition before God.
That is hidden with Christ in God, and our first task is
ensure that we, and those in our own churches, are sharing
in this life, not to obsess over the criteria for other churches to share in it. Meanwhile, we extend them whatever fellowship we can, and exhort them to grow in truth, unity,
and holiness.

---

[24] Richard Hooker, *Lawes of Ecclesiastical Polity*, V.6.1-2.

[25] For more on these elements in Hooker's ecclesiology, and their relationship to his key distinctions of the visible and invisible church, see
my *Richard Hooker: A Companion to His Life and Work* (Eugene, OR: Cascade, 2015), chs. 10-11.

VII:

"A HEAVENLY OFFICE, A HOLY MINISTRY": ORDINATION IN THE ENGLISH REFORMATION

Andre A. Gazal

INTRODUCTION

THE PROTESTANT Reformation in the sixteenth century, in addition to dividing permanently Western Christendom, drastically altered both the devotional and institutional life of the Church in Europe. One of the most conspicuous aspects of this change occurred in the area of polity, wherein alternate forms of ecclesiastical government challenged the longstanding, complex episcopal hierarchy that characterized the late medieval church. Formally established by the magistrates of those regions and locales that officially adopted either Lutheran or Reformed Protestantism, these alternative polities took the form of consistorial government (as was the case with Geneva), oversight by a superintendent (utilized by many Lutheran territories), or direct control by the local civil authorities themselves (which occurred in Zurich). As on the Continent, the Reformation ultimately reshaped significant features of the Church in England.

Throughout the particularly tumultuous and convoluted course of the Reformation in England, the Tudor monarchs and their governments retained the general structure of episcopal governance in the national church. The Elizabethan Settlement, which defined the doctrine, polity, and practice of England's national Protestant church officially confirmed episcopacy as the ecclesiastical government of the realm. In addition to strident and formidable opposition from Continental and English Catholics, the evangelical episcopal establishment faced challenges by other Protestants from within the same church who wanted to replace it with either Presbyterianism or Independency. Defending the national church against Catholic and other Protestant opponents involved vindicating its ministry whose legitimacy rested on the rite of ordination.

Since the twelfth century, ordination, or holy orders, had been numbered among the seven sacraments. Though the origin of the idea of seven sacraments is generally unknown, such a list first appeared in the anonymous *Sentences of Divinity* in 1145.[1] Five of these were common to all Christians: baptism, confirmation, the Eucharist, penance, and extreme unction; however, two were not shared by everyone, marriage and holy orders as the former was reserved only for the laity, and the latter for the clergy. Within the next decade, Peter Lombard incorporated this list into his seminal work, the *Sentences*, where he further developed the theology of the sacraments.[2] The fact that this list appeared in the *Sentences* made it definitive. Moreover, the commentators on Gratian's *Decretum* enumerated seven

---

[1] Jaroslav Pelikan, *The Growth of Medieval Theology (600–1300)* (Chicago: University of Chicago Press, 1978), 209.

[2] Pelikan, *The Growth of Medieval Theology*, 210.

sacraments because of Lombard's influence even though Gratian himself makes no mention of this list.[3] These developments resulted in more elaborately technical definitions for each of the individual sacraments. Theologians, like Lombard, regarded ordination, like marriage, as a sacrament "in which salvation principally consists and is received."[4] Unlike marriage, however, ordination, or holy orders, was "instituted for the sole purpose of preparing and sanctifying the things that are necessary for the sanctification and institution of the other sacraments."[5] Ordination was thus basic to all of the other six sacraments all of which depended on it for their valid administration. Because the sacraments conveyed grace *ex opera operato*, the validity of ordination gravely determined the inherent efficacy of every sacrament. The fear of receiving false sacraments (and hence no grace) due to illegitimate ordinations arguably contributed to the anxiety felt across Western Christendom over the Papal Schism of the late fourteenth and early fifteenth centuries (1378-1415) since an unlawful pope consecrating unsanctioned bishops resulted in empty ordinations which then rendered any sacraments these ordinands would administer useless.

The supernatural grace received through the sacrament of ordination conveyed an indelible spiritual character to the recipient that further empowered him to perform the miraculous act of transubstantiation in the Eucharist, and thus perform the propitiatory sacrifice of the

---

[3] Pelikan, *The Growth of Medieval Theology*, 210.

[4] Lombard, *Sentences*, div. 5. Pr. 2, cited from Pelikan, *Growth of Medieval Theology*, 212.

[5] Hugh of St. Victor, *De Sacramentiis*, I.9.7, cited from Pelikan, *Growth of Medieval Theology*, 212.

Mass. Moreover, being thus invested with this grace via a special receiving of the Holy Spirit at ordination, the priest thereby functions as agent of grace through his administration of all the other six sacraments. The conveying of special grace through ordination established the sacral relationship between the bishop and the other two orders, priest and deacon. The bishop received the fullness of the sacrament of holy orders, which then joined him to the episcopal college and made him the visible head of the particular church entrusted to him, and with it the surrounding diocese. As the successors of the apostles, the bishops shared responsibility for the whole church under the authority of the Pope as the successor of St. Peter and vicar of Christ. Priests were united to the bishops in their sacerdotal dignity, and therefore depended on them in the exercise of their pastoral and sacramental functions. This was because at his ordination, the priest received a portion of the sacramental grace heretofore communicated in its fullness to the bishop. Being joined to the Catholic Church, the Church in England fully maintained within its two provinces of Canterbury and York the ministry of the sacraments inextricably upheld by a sacerdotal priesthood. Providing the clergy the grace to administer grace was the sacrament of ordination.

As the Reformation severed the English Church from papal obedience, and hence from the sacral union of the Roman Church, it proceeded, especially throughout the reigns of Edward VI (r.1547-53), and Elizabeth I (r.1558-1603), to reshape its doctrine, practice, and institutions. In thus transforming the Church of England into a national Protestant Church under the monarch as "Supreme Governor,"[6] evangelical churchmen and theologians reduced the number of sacraments from seven to two, baptism and the Eucharist shorn of the doctrine of transubstantiation, thereby effectively removing the sacramental basis of the Church, and with it the sacerdotal priesthood. Moreover, this drastic change in sacramental theology significantly altered the relationship between bishop and priest, since now the former no longer served as a channel of sacramental grace to the latter through his act of ordination. The removal of ordination from its sacramental status resulted in profound consequences for the ministry.

The following will examine the manner in which some of the major theologians who defined and defended the evangelical doctrine and practice of England's national church sought to retain the distinctive function of ordination in distinguishing a ministry now shorn of its sacerdotal status. This required ultimately the re-establishment of the ministry upon the basis of its didactic role of preaching the Word of God. Specifically, this chapter will investigate the treatment of ordination in relation to the ministry in the work of Archbishop Thomas Cranmer (1489-1556) and Bishop John Jewel (1522-71).

---

[6] Whereas the 1534 Act of Supremacy passed by Parliament under Henry VIII proclaimed the monarch, "Supreme Head" of the Church of England, because of the difficulties presented by the exercise of royal ecclesiastical authority by a woman, the 1559 Act of Supremacy declared the monarch "Supreme Governor" of the Church of England. See Norman Jones, *Faith By Statute, Parliament and the Settlement of Religion, 1559* (London: Royal Historical Society, 1982), 89-144; Andre A. Gazal, *Scripture and Royal Supremacy in Tudor England: The Use of Old Testament Historical Narrative* (Lewiston, NY: Edwin Mellen, Press, 2013), 136-37.

THOMAS CRANMER AND HIS REFORMED ORDINAL

Archbishop Cranmer's most conspicuous contribution to the evangelical reform of ordination was the English Ordinal of 1550.[7] A cursory reading of the document reveals forthright rejection of a sacerdotal priesthood. Not only does the candidate receive bread and cup, but notably, a Bible, which signifies the giving of "authority to preach the Word of God, and to minister the holy sacraments."[8] What this clearly indicates is the candidate being ordained to the ministry of the Word and sacraments, meaning that they are joined together, though distinguishable. Absent from this is any mention of the offering of sacrifices. Readily apparent throughout the service is that the Bible now is the sole instrument of the ministry to which the sacraments are attached. It is not however, the intention of this rite to minimize the importance of the sacraments, but rather to stress their nature as visible words subsumed under the ministry of the Word. Towards the end of the service is a prayer which particularly accents the centrality of preaching and teaching the Word as the essence of ministry:

> Most merciful Father we beseech thee to send
> upon these thy servants thy heavenly blessing;
> that they may be clothed with righteousness,
> and that thy Word spoken by their mouths
> may have such success, that it may never be

---

[7] The Ordinal underwent further revision in 1552 the essentials of which appear in that of 1662 which is in the present *Book of Common Prayer* used officially by the Church of England. It will be this edition that will be referenced and cited throughout this section.

[8] *Book of Common Prayer* (Oxford: Oxford University Press, 1969), 662.

spoken in vain. Grant also, that we may have grace to hear and receive what they shall deliver out of thy most holy Word, or agreeable to the same as the means of our salvation; that in all our words and deeds we may seek thy glory and the increase of thy kingdom through Jesus Christ our Lord. Amen.[9]

The distinctive characteristic of the ministry, as indicated by this prayer, is the purposeful proclamation of the Word as the divinely appointed instrument of securing salvation.

The Ordinal noticeably changes the relationship between the episcopal and priestly orders as evidenced by the service for the consecration of an archbishop or bishop. Binding the ties between bishop and priest is no longer sacramental grace, but the ministry of the Word. As when the candidate was ordained a priest, so now again on the occasion of his consecration he avers that he is "persuaded that the holy Scriptures contain sufficiently all Doctrine required of necessity for eternal salvation faith in Jesus," and that he is "determined out of the same holy Scriptures to instruct the people committed to [his] charge; and to teach or maintain nothing as required of necessity to eternal salvation, but that which [he] shall be persuaded may be concluded and proved the same."[10] The episcopal candidate further affirms that he "faithfully exercise [himself] in the same holy Scriptures, and call upon God by prayer, for the true understanding of the same, so that as [he] may be able by them to teach and exhort with wholesome doctrine, and to withstand and convince the gainsayers."[11] He

---

[9] *Book of Common Prayer*, 662.

[10] *Book of Common Prayer*, 671.

[11] *Book of Common Prayer*, 671.

then promises "to banish and drive away all erroneous and strange doctrine contrary to God's Word, and both privately and openly to call upon and encourage others to the same."[12] As was the case with the priest, the substance of the bishop's ministry is the consistent exposition and defense of the Word of God contained in Holy Scripture.

Like the service of ordination into the priesthood, the rite of consecration of bishop clearly omits any sacerdotal function in this office. In highlighting the ministry of the Word, the liturgy stresses as concomitant the pastoral obligations of the episcopate. These pastoral duties largely consist of setting an example of godliness to others, maintaining discipline in the diocese, "ordaining, sending, or laying hands upon others" as well as demonstrating gentleness and mercy "for Christ's sake to poor and needy people and to all strangers destitute of help."[13] Also as a pastor whose ministry consists fundamentally of preaching the Word, his service extends to protecting the spiritual well-being of God's people:

> Be to the flock of Christ a shepherd, not a wolf; feed them, devour them not. Hold up the weak and heal the sick, bind up the broken, bring again the out-casts, seek the lost. Be so merciful that you be not too remiss; so minister discipline that you forget not mercy: that when the chief Shepherd shall appear you may receive the never-fading crown of glory.

For the bishop as much as the priest, the instrument of ministry is the Scriptures as indicated in the part of the

---

12 *Book of Common Prayer*, 671.

13 *Book of Common Prayer*, 672.

liturgy where the Archbishop gives him a Bible.[14] This aspect of the service highlights the traditional relationship between bishop and priest on the basis of shared ministry; however, rather than participating in the sacerdotal ministry of the diocesan by receiving grace from his fullness thereof via the sacrament of holy orders, the priest joins the bishop's pastoral ministry of the Word. Ordination thus serves the purpose of solemn commission for the dispensation of the Word to which the sacraments conjoined as the visible words of God. What the Ordinal demonstrated theologians explicated in their writings in defense of England's national church particularly as it was codified by the Elizabethan Settlement. The first was John Jewel, Bishop Salisbury and apologist of the Church of England.

JOHN JEWEL'S DOCTRINE OF ORDINATION AND THE PRIESTLY OFFICE

As the first major apologist of the Elizabethan church, John Jewel, Bishop of Salisbury, treated the subjects of ordination and the priestly office within the larger context of his efforts to vindicate the doctrine and practice of England's national Protestant Church against the charges of formidable Catholic critics, especially his former friend and colleague Thomas Harding (1516-72). The works in which Jewel discusses these subjects at length are his *Reply to Harding Answer*, *Apology of the Church of England*, *Defense of the Apology of the Church of England*, and a *Treatise of the Sacraments*.

---

[14] *Book of Common Prayer*, 675.

In order to justify the severance of the Church of England from papal obedience, Jewel impeaches the doctrine of papal primacy over other bishops. Jewel does this by alleging that this doctrine is primarily the result of historical development rather than divine institution. To this effect, he states in the *Reply to Harding*:

> If thou think that the whole church is built only upon Peter, what then wilt thou say of John, the son of thunder, and of every of the apostles? Shall we dare, that the gates of hell shall prevail only against Peter? Or are the keys of the kingdom of heaven given only unto Peter? By these few it may appear, what right the pope hath to claim his authority by God's word, and as M. Harding saith, *de jure divino*.[15]

Because the Scriptures provide no warrant for the pope's claim to authority over other bishops, Harding, the bishop's opponent, cannot maintain the papal claim to be *de jure divino*, or by divine prescription. At this point Jewel identifies the source of papal primacy as custom, and not divine mandate.[16] From here, Jewel candidly applies the same argument to the superiority of bishops to priests: "Let bishops understand that they are greater than the priests, more of custom than of the truth of God's ordinance."[17] Although certainly as a bishop himself, Jewel does not impugn this fact, but rather stresses the conviction that this ministerial relationship is an outgrowth of

---

[15] John Jewel, *The Works of John Jewel*, ed. John Ayre, 4 vols. (Cambridge: The University Press, 1845-50), 1:340.

[16] Jewel, *Works*, 1:340.

[17] Jewel, *Works*, 1:340.

historical circumstances. Furthermore, in the *Defense of the Apology*, Jewel appeals to Erasmus commenting on Jerome to show that the office of bishop, and especially that of metropolitan or archbishop, is the product of historical development and not divine institution: "Erasmus saith, 'the metropolitan had a dignity above other bishops. But he saith not, 'the bishop of Rome had jurisdiction over all bishops throughout the world. In St. Hierome's words time there were metropolitans, archbishops, and others. But Christ appointed not these distinctions of orders from the beginning. These names are not found in all the Scriptures.'"[18] By citing the principal patristic scholar of the sixteenth century, Jewel attempts to corroborate his reference to Jerome to prove that not only papal primacy, but that the various degrees of episcopal office as well as the said office itself as separate from priest are not instituted by Scripture. In arguing for the relatively historical contingency of episcopacy, Jewel further annuls the sacral relationship between bishop and priest in order to underscore the inherent equality of the two degrees by virtue of their shared ministry of the Word with the authority exercised by the former over latter as a matter of ecclesiastical tradition of long antiquity which facilitates proclamation of the Word.

Jewel expounds on ordination itself in his *Treatise of the Sacraments*. In this regard, Jewel unambiguously asserts: "The ministry, holy orders, or ordination is not a sacrament."[19] Rather, "It is a heavenly office, a holy ministry or service."[20] Jewel then describes the essential function of

---

[18] Jewel, *Works*, 3:292.

[19] Jewel, *Works*, 2:1129.

[20] Jewel, *Works*, 2:1129.

the ministry for which ordination sets one apart: "By such as have this office God lighteneth our darkness, he declareth his mind to us, he gathereth together his scattered sheep, and published unto the world the glad tidings of salvation."[21] The principal task of the ministry is the preaching of the Word. At this point, Jewel briefly embarks upon a biblical theology of the preaching office. The Christian ministry parallels the prophetic office. The prophet, Jewel observes, prefaced his message with the formula, "Thus saith the Lord."[22] Yet, in the New Testament, Jewel points out, Christ superseded the prophetic task by becoming "our prophet" who "showed us the will of the Father."[23] In describing Christ's prophetic ministry as ultimately fulfilling the prophetic office, Jewel argues that at no time did Jesus ever institute the ministry as a sacrament. Moreover, Christ did not invest the ministry with the function of offering sacrifices for the forgiveness of sins since Christ as a priest after the order of Melichizedek, accomplished the ultimate sacrifice for humanity's sins.[24] Thus, Christ not only fulfilled the prophetic office, thereby discontinuing it, but even more significantly, the priestly office by means of his sacrificial death once and for all as confirmed with his words exclaimed from the cross, "It is finished."[25]

Since on the basis of Christ's work the ministry is not a sacrament whereby the one ordained performs propitiatory sacrifices, it is, biblically speaking, according to Jewel,

---

[21] Jewel, *Works*, 2:1129.

[22] Jewel, *Works*, 2:1129.

[23] Jewel, *Works*, 2:1129.

[24] Jewel, *Works*, 2:1131.

[25] Jewel, *Works*, 2:1131.

something altogether different. Indeed the holy ministry "standeth in the setting for the ministry of our salvation, both by the preaching of the word of God, and the due and reverened ministration of the sacraments."[26] Like the Ordinal above, Jewel conjoins the sacraments to the preaching of the Word, maintaining the latter to be also a visual declaration of the Word.[27] However, Jewel avers that preaching the Scriptures is the principal duty of the ministry: "The principalist part of this office is to preach repentance; that so we may amend our lives, and be converted unto God."[28] This succinct declaration extends to the power of the keys, which Jewel discusses at length in his *Apology of the Church of England* where he defines them as:

> the preaching of the Gospel [that] offers the merits of Christ and full pardon to such as have lowly and contrite hearts and do unfeignedly repent them, pronouncing unto the same a sure and undoubted forgiveness of their sins and hope of everlasting salvation; or else that the same minister, when any have offended their brothers' minds with some great offence or notable and open crime, whereby they have, as it were, banished and made themselves strangers from the common fellowship and from the body of Christ, then after perfect amendment of such persons, doth reconcile them, and bring them home again,

---

[26] Jewel, *Works*, 2:1131.

[27] Jewel, *Works*, 2:1131.

[28] Jewel, *Works*, 2:1131.

and restore them to the company and unity of the faithful.[29]

Upon equating the preaching of the Scriptures with the keys, Jewel assigns the power of the keys not only equally to all bishops, but all priests. This consignment of the keys to all priests by way of preaching the word as being the essence of ministry for which ordination takes place further equalized practically the orders of bishop and priest. Furthermore, the redefining of ordination by Jewel also shifted the basis of apostolic succession from continuation in office to the inheritance of doctrine whose dissemination is through preaching.[30] Jewel's theology of ordination thus had the effect of maintaining the distinction of the ministry by assigning to it the proclamation of the Word.

CONCLUSION

Thomas Cranmer and John Jewel both represent the overall efforts of the Church of England during the sixteenth century to reform ordination in keeping with the evangelical theology that came to define it. Fundamentally this entailed divesting ordination of its sacramental status while at the same time using it as a means of distinguishing a general order by means of a specific service to the Church. This reformation of ordination involved transforming the ministry from a sacerdotal one in which the priest, having received a portion of sacramental grace by the bishop through a sacrament in order to channel grace through his

---

[29] John Jewel, *Apology of the Church of England*, trans. Ann Bacon, and ed. John Booty (New York: Church Publishing, 2002), 26-27.

[30] Jewel, *Apology*, 25-26.

ministration of the other six to one whose quintessential function was the preaching the Word and administration of the sacraments that were conjoined to it. The change greatly altered the relationship between bishop and priest as it equalized them more by means of a commonly shared ministry of the Word with the distinction being now more a matter of historical development than actual divine prescription even though Jewel as a bishop himself clearly accepted the three traditional orders of bishop, priest, and deacon.[31] The identification of preaching and teaching the Word as the prime function of ministry extended to other areas of ecclesiastical authority. This view of the ministry redefined the power of the keys as the preaching of the Word, and as such placed equally in the hands of priests. This meant that now with respect the major aspect of ecclesiastical power priests were not only equal to one another, but also, at least in theory, to bishops. The prominence preaching the Word as the central task of ministry for which one was now ordained affected the doctrine of apostolic succession as it provided now continuity of teaching as the basis of it even though later in the century and throughout the next, continuity of office would become prime feature of apostolic succession again. In removing its sacramental character from ordination, the evangelical reformation re-sacralized it by adjoining it to the Holy Word.

---

[31] Jewel, *Apology*, 24.

VIII:

EXCURSUS: CHURCH DISCIPLINE AS A WAY OF LOVE[1]

Jordan Ballor

THERE IS a temptation in Christianity that goes something like this: if we can just get our doctrine right, our propositions concerning God and Jesus Christ correct, our theology in proper order, then the rest will take care of itself. This Christian idealism focuses on doctrinal precision, sometimes even to the exclusion of moral or practical conduct. Right belief is all that is necessary in the Christian life, and everything else will either follow necessarily from such belief or it isn't worth accounting for anyway. There is also a version of this temptation that replaces doctrinal rigor and propositional accuracy with emotionalism and identity: it isn't important how you behave or what you believe so long as you feel close to God or simply self-identify as a follower of Christ.

Although these views evince a kind of legalism, to call such modern views "Pharisaical" would do great injustice to the ancient Pharisees. After all, while the Pharisees most

---

[1] This article originally appeared as "Church Discipline as a Public Good" in the Spring 2016 issue of *Comment*, a publication of CARDUS: www.cardus.ca.

---

certainly were concerned about proper belief, they were equally rigorous about conduct. The same group that faulted Jesus for his bad doctrine—"Who can forgive sins but God alone?" (Luke 5:21)—was also worried about his questionable behavior—"Why does your teacher eat with tax collectors and sinners?" (Matt. 9:11). Jesus himself attested to the moral exactitude of the Pharisees: "Unless your righteousness surpasses that of the Pharisees and the teachers of the law, you will certainly not enter the kingdom of heaven" (Matt. 5:20).[2]

The basic problem of the Pharisees wasn't that they were concerned with right doctrine to the exclusion of right practice; it was instead that their improper evaluation of what constituted right practice, their lack of love, led them into hypocrisy and error. Jesus says to them, "Because you give God a tenth of your mint, rue and all other kinds of garden herbs, but you neglect justice and the love of God. You should have practiced the latter without leaving the former undone" (Luke 11:42). Getting discipline right has important implications not only for individual believers and the church itself but for society as well.

HOLINESS AND DISCIPLESHIP

One of the dominant concerns of the Pharisees, flowing out of their devotion to the Torah, had to do with ceremonial purity. Their criticism of Jesus and his disciples not only involved his choice of venue for meals but also related to his lack of concern for ritual cleanliness. Much of the Torah deals with these matters, and the book of Leviticus

---

[2] All Scripture references are to the New International Version unless otherwise noted.

provides great evidence for God's level of concern about even the most seemingly mundane matters.

Chuck Primus, a teacher of Judaica at Notre Dame, once opined that "any religion that doesn't tell you what to do with your pots and pans and genitals can't be interesting."[3] By this standard, the Torah must be judged to be greatly interesting! These claims are developed in the New Testament, which makes more explicit the cosmic scope of God's designs. From the beginning to the end of the Bible, God's claims are universal and comprehensive. When God was present among the Israelites in the times of the tabernacle and then the temple, it was necessary to establish specific and exact guidelines for holiness. Because God is perfect and death, decay, and corruption are alien to him, those who came in proximity to him had to be purified. In the midst of regulations about clean and unclean animals, for example, God provides the basis for such detailed instructions: "I am the Lord, who brought you up out of Egypt to be your God; therefore be holy, because I am holy" (Lev. 11:45). God's chosen people needed to be like him: holy.

The Pharisees were continuing a tradition of understanding of what such holiness entailed. These regulations were given to Moses, and the Pharisees accounted themselves faithful to this tradition. "We are disciples of Moses!" they confessed (John 9:28). The apostle Paul likewise attests to the Pharisees' devotion to the law given to Moses, describing himself as "a Pharisee" in relation to the

---

[3] As quoted in "Christianity: It's Not a Religion, It's an Adventure," in Stanley Hauerwas, *The Hauerwas Reader*, ed. John Berkman and Michael Cartwright (Durham: Duke University Press, 2001), 531.

law and "as to righteousness based on the law, faultless" (Phil. 3:5-6).

The shift in the New Testament has not so much to do with a change in concern for the people's holiness but rather a clarification of the standard by which such holiness is judged and made effective. When the Pharisees appeal to their Mosaic tradition, they do so in explicit contrast to those who follow Jesus. In Jesus' response, the authority for defining the shape and significance for holiness is changed from Moses to Jesus, from the guardian of the estate to the heir himself (Gal. 4:1-2). But the call to holiness, properly understood, remains binding. As Peter writes, "Just as he who called you is holy, so be holy in all you do" (1 Pet. 1:15, NIV).

For the Pharisees, being disciples of Moses meant following the instructions he had passed on, being faithful to the way of life he had communicated to Israel. For Christians, being disciples of Jesus likewise means following his instructions, and being devoted to him as the ultimate authority for true belief and appropriate behavior. Discipleship thus requires discipline, both in terms of objective standards and guidelines provided by the leader and in terms of subjective conformity and obedience provided by the followers.

Perhaps the greatest difference in the discipline and discipleship of the Pharisees from Jesus had to do with the relationship between love and holiness. As Jesus put it, "You have heard that it was said, 'Love your neighbor and hate your enemy.' But I tell you, love your enemies and pray for those who persecute you, that you may be children of your Father in heaven" (Matt. 5:43-45). The ancient Pharisees did discipline without love. Many today want love without discipline. Christ, however, commands both.

DISCIPLINE AND THE EARLY CHURCH

This dynamic between discipline, discipleship, and love can be traced throughout the later history of the church. The *Didache*, one of the earliest documents from the patristic period, outlines the essential characteristics of two paths that can be followed, "two ways, one of life and one of death."[4] The way of life means "First, you shall love God who made you; second, love your neighbor as yourself, and do not do to another what you would not want done to you."[5] The teaching goes on to outline more specific activities demanded by love, both ones that must be avoided (e.g., murder, adultery, pederasty, fornication, theft) and others that must be done. In this latter category there are two things that are particularly significant for the later development of Christian tradition.

First, loving God and loving one's neighbor demand submission and obedience to legitimate authority, outside the church as well as within. With Jesus' resurrection and ascension, the leadership of the institutional church is continued through offices of teaching, preaching, and service. Thus the *Didache* instructs its audience to appoint "bishops and deacons worthy of the Lord, men meek, and not lovers of money, and truthful and proved; for they also render to you the service of prophets and teachers."[6] Paul similar-

---

[4] "Teaching of the Twelve Apostles," in *The Teaching of the Twelve Apostles*, trans. Canon Spence (London: James Nisbet & Co., 1885), 7.

[5] "Teaching of the Twelve Apostles," 9-10.

[6] "Teaching of the Twelve Apostles," 68, 70.

ly instructed Timothy, "Preach the word; be prepared in season and out of season; correct, rebuke and encourage—with great patience and careful instruction" (2 Tim. 4:2). These office-bearers exercise a derived and delegated authority within the church, and thus they ought to be respected and honored.

Second, as the *Didache* continues, Christians must "reprove one another, not in anger, but in peace."[7] Not only are Christians to submit to legitimate authority and be obedient, but they are also to hold one another accountable and responsible for proper conduct. Jesus himself provided the guidance for such mutual accountability and its grounding in the church community in Matthew 18:15-17: "If your brother or sister sins, go and point out their fault, just between the two of you. If they listen to you, you have won them over. But if they will not listen, take one or two others along, so that 'every matter may be established by the testimony of two or three witnesses.' If they still refuse to listen, tell it to the church; and if they refuse to listen even to the church, treat them as you would a pagan or a tax collector."

Even in apostolic times the authority of the earthly delegate sometimes threatened to surpass the identity of the heavenly Lord. Thus Paul observes that among the Corinthian church, "There are quarrels among you." Paul goes on to elaborate: "One of you says, 'I follow Paul'; another, 'I follow Apollos'; another, 'I follow Cephas'; still another, 'I follow Christ'" (1 Cor. 1:11-12). Perhaps there was basic agreement on the substance of the gospel taught by Paul, Apollos, and Cephas. Yet there still must have

---

[7] "Teaching of the Twelve Apostles," 70-71.

been some characteristics that led their followers to identify as their disciples. The Corinthian church experienced
great strife as partisans of different groups vied for control. The Corinthian partisans can be seen as continuing
the spirit of the Pharisees, as each group claimed fidelity to
its authoritative leader, whether Paul, Apollos, Cephas, or
Moses.

This trouble that the Corinthian church faced is illustrative of a basic dynamic related to discipline and discipleship. Standards, guidelines, and instructions both serve to
unite as well as to divide. Discipline unites those who
come together to follow a particular path or leader, distinguishing those followers from the followers of other ways.
If there is some greater good or common cause that unites
different groups, then an element of diversity can be said
to cohere within that larger unity. But such diversity can
also lead to the breakdown of commonality, leading to
division and disunity.

MEDIEVAL ORDERS AND REFORMATION CHURCHES

The historical path from the early church through the medieval period to the time of the Protestant Reformation
illustrates this dynamic. The transition from the ancient era
to the medieval period is marked by, among other things,
the growth and development of religious orders and scholastic traditions. From the Rule of St. Benedict to the Pastoral Rule of Gregory the Great, varied approaches to
Christian identity and social responsibility arose in the
Middle Ages. Great figures of the scholastic intellectual
traditions would later become the basis for wrangling and
disputation. Franciscans and Dominicans would become

two of the more dominant traditions, but other groups, from Augustinians, to Benedictines, to Carthusians (ABC's of religious orders), each worked out their own institutional and cultural paradigms for following Christ. In the best circumstances these various approaches complemented one another and formed a kind of institutional pluralism. But in other cases they jockeyed for intellectual prestige and ecclesiastical influence. Paul's warnings to the church in Corinth had not rooted out the human tendency to align with particular interests and partisan identities.

The breakup of the religious and institutional consensus in the sixteenth century created the need for renewed reflection on the nature of ecclesial identity and discipline. Where the diversity of religious orders and scholastic traditions in the medieval period had grown up under at least a modicum of institutional unity, Protestant reform movements coalesced along confessional and geographic lines to form new and independent church bodies.

The Reformed tradition in particular, along with various Anabaptist and Radical Reformation movements, became closely identified with a disciplinarist vision for church organization. Although John Calvin (1509-1564) is typically credited with defining church discipline as a "mark of the church" along with pure preaching of the gospel and right administration of the sacraments, other influential reformers like Peter Martyr Vermigli (1499-1562) and Jan Łaski (1499-1560) championed an understanding of the church as defined by application of discipline. Vermigli captured the dynamic between love and discipline in advocating a golden mean in the application of various forms of church discipline: "We must take heed that we avoid two extremities, and keep the mean. On the one part, that we use not a fair and flattering speech, whereby we rather nourish vices than remove them. On the other part, that we use not over rough and raw admonition: lest we rather turn a man from salvation, than lead him unto it."

This emphasis on discipline as characteristic of the true church of Christ would be codified in church orders and confessional documents. As the Belgic Confession (1561) of the Reformed tradition relates, members of the church are to keep the church's unity in part "by submitting to its instruction and discipline, by bending their necks under the yoke of Jesus Christ, and by serving to build up one another" (art. 28). The marks of the church, which include the practice of "church discipline for correcting faults" (art. 29), are intended to help believers discern and recognize the true church.

DISCIPLINE AND DISTINCTIVE CHURCHES

Discipline is thus a distinctive of the Christian church. But as the examples of the ancient Pharisees indicate, Christian discipline is further distinguished by Christian love. Jesus instructs his followers, "By this everyone will know that you are my disciples, if you love one another" (John 13:35). But our love must not be the veneer of emotionalism that merely approves of anything and everything. Christian love is a tough-minded love, a love in the midst of mess and trial. It is love for friends as well as enemies, and involves the ability to discern the appropriate ways to love in concrete situations.

There's an ancient debate about whether the word *religion* is derived from the verb "to repeat" (*relegere*) or "to bind together" (*religare*). The emphasis in the first case is vertical and has to do with true worship, the accuracy and faithfulness of religious observance. In the second case, the emphasis is horizontal, and describes the social cohesion that attends to religious activity. But both elements are necessary and stand or fall together. As with the two great love commandments, concern to give right worship to God must come to expression in love of neighbor. And no religious community can exist without devotion and proper orientation to God.

Perhaps the gravest threat to discipleship and discipline today is the idea of the autonomous and sovereign individual self. We moderns have a big problem with authority, either recognizing it or submitting to it. The social realities of church attendance and membership today largely mean that if there is something we dislike or find uncomfortable about a particular congregation, then we simply move along until we find one that meets our desires. The greatest obstacle to church discipline and Christian discipleship today, then, is the lack of self-discipline and commitment to a church community by churchgoers themselves. This is, in fundamental ways, a deeply countercultural diagnosis. But as David Wells observes in *God in the Wasteland*, when "the church is authentic, when it is true to its nature as a possession of God, its cultural irrelevance becomes a very real virtue."[8]

A church of disciples united in love becomes a foretaste of the kingdom and the soul of the broader society. As the apostle Peter urges, "Live such good lives among the pagans that, though they accuse you of doing wrong,

---

[8] David F. Wells, *God in the Wasteland: The Reality of Truth in a World of Fading Dreams* (Grand Rapids: Eerdmans, 1994), 224.

they may see your good deeds and glorify God on the day he visits us" (1 Pet. 2:12). The Bible uses the images of salt, light, and leaven to describe the impact of the moral and spiritual effects of the Christian church, distinguished by love and discipline, on the world.

If the Pharisees erred on the side of discipline without love, modern libertines err on the side of love without discipline. The same Jesus who warned against the legalistic and hypocritical leaven of the Pharisees likewise warned against the licentiousness of those who, out of a misplaced and mistaken understanding of love, would do away with law and discipline. In this way Jesus warns the church in Thyatira, "Nevertheless, I have this against you: You tolerate that woman Jezebel, who calls herself a prophet. By her teaching she misleads my servants into sexual immorality and the eating of food sacrificed to idols" (Rev. 2:20).

So we see that Jesus, no less than the book of Leviticus, does indeed concern himself with, to use Chuck Primus's phrase again, "pots and pans and genitals." Stanley Hauerwas uses Primus's formula as a way of introducing religion's binding claims on human beings. Speaking particularly about sexual responsibility, Hauerwas writes that Christians "do not believe that we have a right to do whatever we want with our bodies. We do not believe that we have a right to our bodies because when we are baptized we become members of one another; then we can tell one another what it is that we should and should not do with our bodies."[9] The same goes for pots and pans, as Hauerwas continues, as well as for all the other areas of life.

God disciplines those whom he loves (Prov. 3:12; Heb. 12:6; Rev. 3:19); when he disciplines us in the church,

---

[9] "Abortion, Theologically Understood," in *The Hauerwas Reader*, 609.

can we bear such correction without running away? As Paul puts it, "You are not your own; you were bought at a price. Therefore honor God with your bodies" (1 Cor. 6:19-20). The Heidelberg Catechism opens with this theme and expands it to apply not only to our bodies but also to our souls: "I am not my own, but belong—body and soul, in life and in death—to my faithful Savior, Jesus Christ." We owe it to one another to hold each other accountable, to rebuke one another in love, to hold fast to what we have been taught, and thus to disciple others in the discipline of Jesus Christ.

PART IV:
PROTESTANT ECCLESIOLOGY TODAY

IX:
PROTESTANT ECCLESIOLOGY AS GOOD THEORY
Andrew Fulford

INTRODUCTION

WHAT makes a good theory? Though it's certain that philosophers could debate this endlessly (and what can't they?), for our purposes we can limit the criteria to three. First, it fits with the clearly evident facts of the matter. Second, it resolves puzzlement over unclear issues, and adds none through incoherence. Third, it does not offer multiple explanations for data where one is sufficient.

Protestant ecclesiology isn't merely an interesting historical artifact; it's a good theory. In fact, this essay will argue that it's the best theory we have. Resting on the cardinal insight of justification by faith alone, magisterial Protestant soteriology is transparent to the clear biblical and real-world evidence about the *ecclesia*, and elegantly dissolves the tensions about it. In order to make this case, this essay will first present the scriptural data, and then show how Protestantism makes sense of some common, real, and difficult pastoral cases.

FAITH

Faith Justifies Us

At the opening of Romans 5, Paul concludes from his argument thus far: "Therefore, having been justified by faith, we have peace with God through our Lord Jesus Christ."[1] Comparing this text with 3:25-26 and 4:16-18, Luther's insight into the concept of justification is undeniable: it is a judicial declaration contrary to condemnation. But the inquisitive mind naturally wants to know why the instrument of faith is sufficient to justify us. Thankfully, Paul illuminates the reader on that question just before this verse. As NT Wright points out in his commentary on Romans,[2] in 4:17-21, the apostle describes the attitude of the patriarch in striking contrast with his image of the human soul in Romans 1:20-21. There, human beings knew God but did not glorify him, and as a result their minds were darkened and their hearts hardened. Abraham, however, recognized God's omnipotence and trustworthiness, and believed the Lord's promise. In the former case, human beings were condemned, and in the latter, one man was justified. According to the apostle, the beginning of the world's problems arrived when human beings stopped thinking of God as the evidence directed them to, and in God's plan to make all things new, salvation begins with the human mind and heart turning back to God in self-forgetful trust based on knowledge of him. The site of the fundamental problem in the universe is also the place where redemption is first applied.

---

[1] All quotes from the Bible are from the *New American Standard Bible* (La Habra: Foundation Press, 1995).

[2] N. T. Wright, *Acts, Romans, 1 Corinthians*, vol. 10 of *The New Interpreter's Bible* (Nashville: Abingdon Press), 500.

The Object of Faith

But trust in what, exactly? In Romans 4:1-12 Paul argues that righteousness is counted to both Jewish and Gentile believers. Later in 11:17-21, he argues that unbelieving Israelite branches were cut off from faithful patriarchal tree because of their unbelief, and that Gentile branches are now part of the tree because of their faith. The implication is that all living branches on this tree share a common faith. Yet in 10:9, it seems clear that part of saving faith for Paul is belief in the resurrection of Jesus of Nazareth. This poses a prima facie difficulty, as Abraham and his pre-Christian descendants could not have had the exact same propositional content for their faith.

This difficulty increases when we turn to the epistle to the Hebrews. At the end of chapter 10 (vv. 36-39), the writer discusses saving faith and then turns to write his famous "hall of faith" chapter. Through the course of chapter 11, we learn that to please God one must believe he exists and rewards those who seek him (v. 6), that all those in this roll were commended through their faith (v. 39), and that they were yet not made perfect apart from New Covenant believers (v. 40). These individuals are thus part of one group that has saving faith in common, like Paul says in Romans. At the same time, what they believed was not propositionally identical: Abel (v. 4), Abraham (vv. 10, 13-16), and Moses (vv. 26-27) could not have faith, e.g., in a descendent of David, since they didn't know of a David. Moving beyond Hebrews, we can see that in Adam's day the content of saving faith was Genesis 3:15, and in Abraham's it was Genesis 12:5. During Jesus' ministry it was "the kingdom of God is at hand" (in him) (Mark 2:15). After his ascension, the content of saving faith, sometimes called "the Gospel," could vary in size from the books whose titles possess that term, to the idea that Jesus is Lord and that God raised him from the dead (Rom. 10:9), or Christ and him crucified (1 Cor. 2:2), or a combination of the two (1 Cor. 15:3-4), or simply Christ (Col. 1:27, cf. 2:3-4).

At this point it is useful to keep Hebrews 11:6's basic point in mind as we consider some other texts. Isaiah 66:2 and Psalm 51:17 similarly state that what God ultimately commends is a humble and contrite heart towards God. And on the contrary side, James 2:19 tells us: "You believe that God is one. You do well; the demons also believe, and shudder." Demons, lacking saving belief, do not lack orthodox content. In the traditional definition of the parts of faith, consisting of the content believed, the assent to it, and personal trust, the demons lack only the last part, and it makes the difference between salvation and condemnation. What they crucially lack is not an intellect in contact with reality, but a rightly ordered will. As Richard Muller says about John Calvin's view of the matter: "It is the intellect that knows and recognizes its knowledge to be true and assents to that truth; only when the heart—that is, the will and its affections—grasps that truth in trust can the truth be appropriated savingly by the individual."[3]

We can perhaps now see the hinge point that holds all these cases in common. First, all saving faith is aimed toward God as he promises salvation to those who believe. That is, simply believing that God condemns us in our sinfulness is not sufficient for saving faith. At the same time, that God's special revelation consistently includes a

---

[3] Richard A. Muller, *The Unaccommodated Calvin* (New York: Oxford University, 2000), 170.

promise of grace is evident from Genesis 3:15 to John 3:16. And second, while the believing saints have differing propositional content in their saving faith, it nevertheless has in common a will that humbly trusts in God and his promises as good for us; the demons, on the other hand, have accurate propositional content, but a will that opposes rather than trusts him. The demonic beings are of course not alone; this is precisely the attitude of heart that we have already seen in Romans 1, where humans suppressed their accurate knowledge of God and in turn were spiritually lost. And in sum, saving faith is such because it is the turning of the will back towards God in love and trust. This direction of will can entail different belief content depending on what God has revealed and promised to a person, but whatever he has shown, a person with this kind of volition will believe it, because they trust the Revealer. Herman Bavinck sums up the larger point we've been making so far:

> In studying the relation between faith and theology, we need to frame the question properly. It should not be: what is the minimum of truths a person must know and hold as true to be saved? Leave that question to Rome, and let Catholic theology decide whether to that end two or four articles are needed. Admittedly, Protestant theology, in the theory of "fundamental articles," has given the impression of wanting to take that road. But it ended with the acknowledgement that it did not know the magnitude of God's mercy and therefore could not measure the amount of knowledge that is necessarily inherent in a sincere faith. ... Faith on the side of the Reformation ... is special (*fides specialis*)

with a particular central object: the grace of God in Christ. Here an arithmetic addition of articles, the knowledge of which and the assent to which is necessary for salvation, was no longer an option. Faith is a personal relation to Christ; it is organic and has put aside quantitative addition. ... On the side of the Reformation, faith is trust in the grace of God and hence no longer calculable.[4]

Faith Unites Us to Jesus

As many in recent years have noted, for Calvin at least, justification by faith is of a piece with union with Christ. In this regard, Calvin is a faithful interpreter of scripture. While earlier in the letter Paul speaks of believers receiving no condemnation, in Romans 8:1 he awards that blessing to those "in Christ Jesus". In Ephesians 2:5-9, the apostle explains that God saved believers through faith, making them alive in Christ. In Ephesians 3:4-7, he further writes:

> By referring to this, when you read you can understand my insight into the mystery of Christ, which in other generations was not made known to the sons of men, as it has now been revealed to His holy apostles and prophets in the Spirit; to be specific, that the Gentiles are fellow heirs and fellow members of the body, and fellow partakers of the promise in Christ Jesus through the gospel, of which I was made a minister, according to the gift of God's grace which was given to me according to the working of His power.

---

[4] Herman Bavinck, *Reformed Dogmatics*, trans. John Vriend, and ed. John Bolt (Grand Rapids: Baker Academic, 2008), 1:614.

Through the gospel, i.e., faith in it, Gentiles are made fellow heirs, fellow members of the body (cf. Rom. 12:4; 1 Cor. 1:2, 6:15), fellow partakers of the promise in Christ Jesus. Similarly, Paul reminds the Corinthians (1 Cor. 4:15) that he became their father in Christ through their believing reception of his proclamation of the gospel. In short, believers are in Christ by their faith, just as much as they are justified by it. And insofar as they are in Christ, as they are His body, then they are *ipso facto* members of the church, for the apostle also regards the body of Christ and the church as coterminous (Eph. 1:22-23, emphasis added): "And He put all things in subjection under His feet, and gave Him as head over all things to *the church, which is His body*, the fullness of Him who fills all in all." This church or body is also, as such, one (2:15), holy (1:1; 2:19), built on the apostles or apostolic (2:20), and catholic in the sense that it is not confined to one place or people group (2:17-18).

Implication: Invisible

As a disposition of intellect and will, faith is intrinsically as invisible as those faculties. This point is confirmed by the apostle, if biblical proof were needed for it (1 Cor. 2:11a): "For who among men knows the thoughts of a man except the spirit of the man which is in him?" It is for this reason that the Protestant tradition has affirmed the concept of the invisible church. Not, to be clear, because believers as human beings are invisible, but because membership in the church is accomplished by faith, which is invisible *per se*, though as we will see, its effects are not. And because faith itself is a gift of God (Eph. 2:8; Phil. 1:29), Protestants have affirmed that only God ultimately controls who is a part of the invisible church, though humans can perform sacraments and other outwardly good actions.

WORKS

Faith Working Through Love

The idea that faith generates effects is mentioned in numerous places. Faith works through love (Gal. 5:6), it issues in love (1 Tim. 1:5), it has works (2 Thess. 1:11), it is completed by works (James 2:22), and anything that does not issue from it is sin (Rom. 14:23). Similar things are said of repentance. As the negative turning away that correlates with the positive turning toward faith in God (Mark 1:15; Acts 26:20), it is an attitude of the heart which issues in action: John the Baptist calls for fruit (Luke 3:8), and Paul for deeds (Acts 26:20), in keeping with repentance. And given that faith is a disposition held by people, it is not surprising to also find texts that link fruit to the nature of people. John the Baptist calls for his hearers to be trees that bring forth good fruit (equivalent with the fruit of repentance, Luke 3:9), and Jesus continues the charge (cf. Matthew 3, 7, 12; John 15).

As a negative corollary, various texts indicate that people who lack these works lack the faith that produces them. James 2:14, 17 arguably contains the clearest of them: "What good is it, my brothers, if someone says he has faith but does not have works? Can that faith save him? ... So also faith by itself, if it does not have works, is dead." The opening rhetorical question anticipates a negative answer, and the metaphors of faith as dead that follow remind us of the analogy we have already seen between faith and a living tree that produces fruit. Other texts make this point: 2 Pet. 2:22 describes the sin of apostates as rooted in what was their nature all along, Jesus' parables of the soil (Matt. 13/Mark 4/Luke 8) explain failure to bear fruit through the pre-existing nature of the soil when it received the seed, and 1 John 3:6 is probably starkly repeating this judgment.

At this point we run into another tension. The texts so far paint a simple picture: faith produces good works, and if they are absent, so is the faith. Yet the NT is also realistic about the ongoing presence of sin in the lives of believers. For example, after describing the experience of "the body of death" in Rom. 7:17-24, Paul affirms in 8:10 that believers still possess it. In 1 John 1:8-2:2 we see clear indications that believers can at least possibly sin, and that if they say they have no sin, that they are lying. Matt. 6:9, 12-15 has Jesus instructing his disciples to regularly pray for forgiveness, assuming that they will need to. Innumerable exhortations to believers to flee from sin throughout scripture confirm this doctrine: the writers anticipate the possibility of believers sinning, and exhort them not to do so. Most vividly, in 2 Cor. 2:5-8 Paul pleads with the Corinthians to restore a repentant man who was under the discipline of the community. Given that Jesus taught his church to only do this after contumacy was evident (Matt. 18:15-20), we can assume that this is a person who was clearly in persisting sin. Yet all the same, Paul calls on the believers of that church to restore him to fellowship as a believer along with them.

But the tension is not irresolvable. We have already encountered a hint towards its dissolution, in the form of the metaphor of faith as a tree that produces fruit. Natural living substances by definition have characteristic ways of being and action that correspond to their natures, yet observation shows us that these ways of being can be interrupted and damaged, such that defective effects are produced instead of good ones. In a sermon aimed at comforting those lacking assurance of salvation, Richard Hooker applies this metaphysical insight to one fruit of the Spirit, joy:

> Hence an error groweth, when men in heaviness of spirit suppose they lack faith, because they find not the sugared joy and delight which indeed doth accompanie faith, but so as a separable accident, as a thing that may be removed from it... .[5]

A tree may still be a good tree even if it sometimes produces defective fruit, and faith will generate joy, and good works, though it may sometimes be mixed with sadness and sin.

Yet, in coming to know the natural world, we proceed by way of observing a thing's operations to knowing what kind of thing it is. That is, the kind of thing that characteristically is and acts in such a way. Characteristic action can allow for exceptions, but when something we might have originally thought to be exceptional turns out to be the rule, we have an indication that we are observing a different thing, with a different nature, than we thought at first. The Bible assumes this natural process of coming to know natures. Occasions of sin, even occasions of habitual sin eventually ended with repentance, are different than regular pattern of sin without any sign of good fruit in keeping with repentance. They are different precisely in

---

[5] Richard Hooker, *A learned and comfortable sermon of the certaintie and perpetuitie of faith in the elect especially of the prophet Habakkuks faith*, 2nd ed. (Oxford: Joseph Barnes, 1612), 8.

how they point to a different nature, a different internal state, a different kind of faith: one with the humble will that makes it saving faith, and the other without.

This is compatible with a great deal of complexity in the life of the believer. Because of indwelling sin, because of the partial darkness of intellect that results from it, and because grace begins with saving faith and not a complete renovation of all habits, there are many causes of sin inside the true believer. God may and does in some times and places immediately remove certain habits from believers; but in other cases he does not, and requires a more cooperative process of rooting out sinful dispositions. In that category, sins of ignorance may persist for a while; yet when God illumines the believer to recognize them, the changed volition will oppose it. This does not mean it will do so with absolute constancy or that this will result in an immediate elimination of the disposition; that will depend on the force of will, mental health, wisdom in strategy, and ultimately the sanctifying grace of God. But it will at least resolve not to simply give up the fight to want to obey.

And so we find the answer to our question. When a soul can say truthfully that it "joyfully concur[s] with the law of God in the inner man" (Rom. 7:21), even if it sins (cf. Rom. 8:10), if at minimum it can say it has not willed to give up the fight against sin, it possesses a saving faith; if on the other hand it is set on the flesh, hostile toward and unable to submit to God's law (Rom. 8:7), then even if it affirms orthodox ideas or produces outwardly good works, it does not possess saving faith.

Implication: Visible

If the invisibility of the disposition of faith entails the "invisible church", the outward operations that properly follow from it entail the reality of the "visible church." As before, the idea here is not that there are non-overlapping churches; the point is instead that only God can see with certainty who has saving faith, while outwardly some can falsely appear to possess it, and others can at times appear not to have it when they actually do. Nevertheless, as we will see, Scripture teaches that certain actions will reliably follow from saving faith, and these serve as marks of the church. Given that faith is a gift of God only, and that it alone makes one a member of Christ's body, the church, none of these marks are constitutive of the church as such. Rather, they are descriptive of those properties that naturally (and so, for the most part) follow from faith.

Marks of the Church: The Word and Profession of Faith

Protestants have traditionally enumerated two or three "marks" of the church. The first of these marks is the true "word," which referred to the true doctrine that a church was teaching. We will return to the teaching of the word below; for now, we will dwell on the profession of it. As noted above, Romans 10:10 makes profession of faith an instrument of salvation, and in Matt. 12:36-37, Jesus warns that people will be condemned or justified based on the words they speak. This raises yet another tension to consider: in the language of Romans, if believing in the heart makes one justified, how can confessing with the mouth make one saved? Isn't one already saved at that point? One could raise a similar question about the petition of the

Lord's prayer (Matt. 6:12) that instructs followers of Jesus to regularly ask God for forgiveness.

Here it is useful to recall that the NT speaks of faith saving people in an ongoing way. For example, 1 Peter 1:5 says that Christians "by God's power are being guarded through faith for a salvation ready to be revealed in the last time," and Gal. 2:20 along with Hebrews 11 speak of them living by faith in an ongoing way. Faith does not merely save at the outset, but all along the Christian life serves to keep the pilgrim church on the path to final salvation, and in that sense saves them progressively through life. Understanding this function of faith, we can then see how scripture could teach that certain speech acts save those who make them: because, as is clear in a profession of faith, such acts express saving faith, God commends them accordingly. He grants continuing salvation to continuing faith, considered as enduring disposition and considered in discrete moments. And thus scripture speaks of moments of profession as resulting in salvation.

Marks of the Church: Baptism

The second Protestant mark of the church is the true sacraments: Baptism and the Lord's Supper. Scripture itself does not call these ritual actions "sacraments," but longstanding tradition has labelled them as such. In Matt. 28:19 and Acts 2:38 we see baptism commanded (indirectly and directly) for followers of Jesus. Given that humble faith naturally produces obedience to God, those who have faith will in general also seek to be baptized, and thus baptism will be a mark that picks out Christians from among the human race.

In 1 Peter 3:21 the apostle Peter says: "baptism now saves you—not the removal of dirt from the flesh, but an appeal to God for a good conscience—through the resurrection of Jesus Christ." The NASB translation has the word "appeal" where others have argued "pledge" would be more accurate.[6] For our purposes either could be true. Baptism is thus both a command and either an appeal or a pledge, and it saves those who receive it. Along with John 3:5, 1 Peter 3:21 is probably the most cited verse to support the idea of baptismal regeneration, and thus raises a problem similar to the previous two we have addressed: if faith justifies and saves, what can be left for baptism to do? But the solution for the previous problem applies just as much in the present case. As obedience to a command of the Lord, and as either an appeal or a pledge to God, the ritual assumes the presence of faith on the part of the recipient. (We will set aside the case of infant baptism, to be discussed briefly below.) And as an act of faith, God responds to it with saving grace, though not for the first time. Moreover, as the ritual which visibly initiates a person into the visible church, a body of people that professes to be saved, it is especially fitting to speak of the act as saving the person who undertakes it. Nevertheless, Protestants need not say that a person is damned prior to baptism, since saving faith precedes it (at least in the case of adult converts).

Marks of the Church: The Lord's Supper

As with baptism, the Lord commanded his followers to participate in the Lord's Supper in remembrance to, or as a

---

[6] E.g., Everett Ferguson, *Baptism in the Early Church* (Grand Rapids: Wm. B. Eerdmans, 2009), 192.

memorial of, him (1 Cor. 11:23-25). And so as with profession of faith and baptism, this is yet another obedient action that saving faith will naturally perform, making it a practice that marks out the church from human race. In addition to being a command, Paul also says that participation functions as a proclamation of the death of the Lord until he returns again. The judgment that follows upon those who take the Supper unworthily also reveals it to be a covenant ratifying meal (1 Cor. 11:25-31), as covenants include oaths, and oaths call down curses on those who break them.[7] Many interpreters have also argued that Jesus' discourse in John 6 on eating his flesh and blood are also allusive of the Supper. If we accept this reading for the sake of argument, we have another example of scripture speaking of certain actions being causes of salvation, as Jesus says in 6:53-54: "Truly, truly, I say to you, unless you eat the flesh of the Son of Man and drink His blood, you have no life in yourselves. He who eats My flesh and drinks My blood has eternal life, and I will raise him up on the last day."

We can explain the soteriological function of the Supper as we did with profession of faith and baptism. The Supper is a case of obedience to a command, an oath of allegiance, a memorial or remembrance, and a proclamation. It is not difficult to see that all of these are done as an expression, or on the supposition of saving faith. This is

---

[7] Cf. Roy E. Ciampa and Brian S. Rosner, *The First Letter to the Corinthians*, The Pillar New Testament Commentary (Grand Rapids: Wm. B. Eerdmans, 2010), 474. Also see Stephen C. Perks, *The Christian Passover: Agape Feast or Ritual Abuse?* (Taunton: Kuyper Foundation, 2012) for an extended discussion of what the rite as handed down by Jesus ought to actually look like, and how it would affect our church practice if we did as he directed.

especially evident in the symbolism of the Supper, which represents the death of Jesus for the forgiveness of sins, offered freely to all who will receive. And once again, we know the Lord responds to such faith with salvific favor, initially and continuously.

Discipline

Anabaptists and some Reformed thinkers added a third mark of the church, variously described as "holiness" or "discipline" or "love", based on texts such as Hebrews 12:14 or John 13:34-35: "A new commandment I give to you, that you love one another, even as I have loved you, that you also love one another. By this all men will know that you are My disciples, if you have love for one another." Lutherans and other Reformed thinkers have tended not to include this as a mark, largely because of the logic of *sola fide*.[8] Nevertheless we need not reject the third mark, if we continue with our understanding of the marks of the church as descriptive and not constitutive of the church, following always or for the most part from saving faith, but not being coordinate independent instruments of salvation, nor necessarily present in every moment of a saved soul's life. Since faith naturally works through love (Gal. 5:6; 2 Thess. 1:11), good works and love will be a regular sign of saving faith, and membership in the church, in the life of believers.

The whole life of the corporate church flows from what we have seen thus far, and can be viewed as an aspect

---

[8] See Jordan Ballor and W. Bradford Littlejohn, "European Calvinism: Church Discipline," *European History Online (EGO)*, March 25, 2013, http://www.ieg-ego.eu/ballorj-littlejohnw-2013-en. for further discussion on the varieties of conceptions of church discipline in the Reformed tradition (accessed on May 25, 2017).

of the third mark (though not in abstraction from the other two). To begin, the common union with Christ by faith creates one body out of all believers, as we have already seen. Furthermore, Christ also dwells in believers (Rom. 8:11; Col. 1:27). For this reason, Jesus' promise to be with even two or three gathered in his name (Matt. 18:20) should not surprise us. And for the same reason, neither should Paul's teaching that the body of Christ has a common good (1 Cor. 12:7). As people who love rightly and do good, then, Christians will seek to uphold the common good intertwined with their personal good.

There are various ways that this is done in practice. In concrete reality, the church is numerous and spread across the globe, making regular meetings of the entire body practically impossible. Nevertheless, while such meetings may be impossible, practical demonstrations of love are not. Thus we see, for example, Paul seeking in various trips and letters to take up funds from Gentile churches to support Jewish churches experiencing famine (e.g., Rom. 15:22-33).

Yet, where meetings are possible, many reasons require more from Christians in a geographic location than those spread across different ones. First, performing baptism and the Lord's Supper require more than an individual participant. Second, as with the global church, so even more so must the local group care materially for one another (e.g., James 1:27; 1 John 3:17-18). Third, God's glory is increased when he answers the prayers of many rather than just an individual (cf. 2 Cor. 1:11), which requires the sharing of knowledge about needs, and coordinated prayer, among many. And fourth, the reality of indwelling sin, of human forgetfulness, and of unsaved members of the visible church makes the need for regular meetings crucial, as scripture confirms (Heb. 10:25). This is because individual Christians need to be reminded, encouraged, exhorted, and warned as their personal state of soul requires.[9] In some cases, in fact, such individuals need to be told that, in the judgment of the body, their actions show they are no longer members of it (e.g. 1 Cor. 5). This is also true when unsaved members reveal their lack of faith through a consistent absence of holiness and love in the sense we have defined it. At the same time, reason shows that Christians cannot spend all of their time in these types of meetings. This point implies what was meant traditionally by the first mark of the church, which is that the doctrine taught by a local church must be true (since to properly build up one another, Christians must share God's word with each other).

It is important to see that, from what has been said, the church can exist, at least temporarily, in places without leaders. This point is rooted in *sola fide*. If human beings are justified and united to Christ, and his body, by faith, then it does not depend upon the intermediating work of human leaders for its very existence. Though Roman Catholicism has read texts like Matt. 16:18-19 as contradicting this idea, in fact the text does not do so. At minimum, this is because the same promise made to Peter in 16:19 is made to all groups of 2-3 disciples in general in 18:18, but

---

[9] See Carl Mosser, "Torah Instruction, Discussion, and Prophecy in First-Century Synagogues," in *Christian Origins and Hellenistic Judaism*, ed. Stanley E. Porter and Andrew W. Pitts, vol. 2 of *Early Christianity in Its Hellenistic Context* (Leiden: Brill, 2013) for an historical survey of how first century Jews and Christians actually did this: i.e., synagogue services consisted of a short running commentary on a biblical text given by a teacher, followed by an extended time of community discussion, which in Christian circles also included the exercise of charismatic gifts.

no one can realistically claim that the all judgments made by such groups are infallible.[10] What this means is that an assumed qualification must be present in these texts, to the effect that it is only when the judgments of Christians accurately reflect the judgments of heaven, logically rooted in the confession of Christ's Lordship, that heaven will bind or loose (or have already done so).

Yet, for a number of reasons, love for the common good of the body in a local context will also lead to creation of church offices. First, it is a commonly accepted observation that a group of individuals can achieve greater profit if the group engages in some degree of division of labor and specialization. This is true even when some of the labor involved is in instruction and care of souls. Prudence alone would thus highly suggest the creation of church offices, staffed by people who have more experience and skill in these practices necessary for the common and personal good. Second, because the church grows and lives in history, there is inevitably always a variation in levels of maturity between believers in any given location. Once again, prudence would suggest making the more mature responsible for the edification of the less mature. Third, scripture tells us that Christ regularly gives gifts to his body in the form of people with gifts for the building

---

[10] Matt 16:19 and 18:18 are controversial for a number of reasons, not least including the meaning of the future periphrastic perfects. D. A. Carson "Matthew," in *Matthew and Mark*, ed. David E. Garland and Tremper Longman, III, Revised ed., vol. 9 of *The Expositor's Bible Commentary* (Grand Rapids: Zondervan, 2010), 422, notes that sacerdotalism is not necessarily avoided regardless of whether they are understood as English futures ("will be bound") or future perfects ("will have been bound"). The explicitly unqualified connection between the activity of earth and heaven is the source of the sacerdotal mistake, but there is good reason in context to provide qualification.

up of the body (Eph. 4:11), and it encourages members of churches to submit to their leaders (e.g., 1 Cor. 16:15-16; Heb. 13:17).

Implication: Organic and Institutional

The preceding points require an organic/institutional distinction. When the Lord by various means requires his body to periodically meet together, to regularly speak the word, baptize, celebrate the Lord's Supper, to discipline the flock, and to appoint wise leaders, he directs the church to create persisting institutions. At the same time, when scripture requires Christians to scatter to do their temporal work and earn a living (1 Thess. 4:11), it requires an organic church, united by faith while separated by space and activity.

PRACTICAL IMPLICATIONS

With this outline of a Protestant theory of the church, we can now turn to practical applications of it, to show how it helps us make realistic and accurate judgments in lived experience.

What About the Children of Believers?

One group of questions surrounds how the children of believers should be treated by the church. Churches descended from the magisterial Reformation have argued for and against paedocommunion and paedobaptism,[11] and

---

[11] On paedocommunion, the differences between theologians such as Musculus and Calvin are relatively well known among Reformed academics; regarding paedobaptism, while some have argued that anti-paedobaptism puts one outside the Reformed pale, this is at least contestable, and has been well disputed by Matthew Bingham in his 2016

amongst those who agree on practice in these matters, often they still provide divergent justifications for that practice. Space does not permit much comment on this subject, except to say that the present author holds to a dual practice view on both baptism and communion, and believes it to be consistent with the theory presented above.

What About Christians Who Disagree?

One issue the Protestant theory is well equipped to discuss is the pluriformity of Christian confessions. This may seem amusing to some readers, as one longstanding Roman Catholic objection to Protestant doctrine is the apparent splintering in the church it has fostered. In opposition, they claim that an international clerical institution, headed by the Pope, is practically required by the obligation of Christian unity. Protestants reply that the unity scripture affirms as real exists even amongst differences, and that such an international magisterium is unnecessary and unhelpful.

Starting with the second point first, the Protestant theory can make several arguments. First, the well known social ethics principle of subsidiarity would obviate the need for an international organization to make local decisions, which could better be determined by those with more local knowledge. Second, while it would be ideal for all Christian doctrine and discipline to be both right and commonly respected by other churches, given sin and its consequences, it is more prudent for the goals of the whole church for local churches to allow some disagreements, rather than wasting time endlessly debating matters

---

Convivium Irenicum presentation "'Reformed Baptist': Anachronistic Oxymoron or Useful Signpost?"

unlikely to be resolved in the near future. Paul's warning in various cases against debating supports this contention (e.g., Rom. 14:1; 1 Tim. 6:4; Titus 3:9-10). This solution is much like the one that has been prudently achieved by the human race on the international political level, with a common regime of international law mutually affirmed by various sovereign nation states. Third, the dangers of giving so much ecclesiastical power to one person are easy to imagine, and prudence requires heeding avoidable dangers in forming regimes. Fourth, the nature of the church does not require such a leader, and neither do any biblical texts. The most commonly adduced passage, Matt. 16:18, does not mandate or entail a perpetual Petrine office throughout church history. Fifth, the existence of such an office cannot actually eliminate the causes of the differences in the church today. The fact of the Great Schism and the Reformation are proof of this.

Returning to the Protestant explanation of the differences consistent with scriptural church unity, the basic point is this: all differences in doctrine can be explained by ignorance of the full scope of scripture's teaching in intellect, or a bad will which persistently rejects known truth. (Traditionally this insight was reflected in the distinction between material and formal heresy.) Sometimes ignorance can be exploited, intentionally or not, by an incorrect tradition or teacher. Nevertheless, the points we have made about indwelling sin in real Christians and false professors in the church enable Protestants to deal realistically with pluriformity. The former point allows us to recognize that even saved Christians can be mistaken due to ignorance, doubt temporarily (Jude 1:22; cf. the case of Thomas), or profess falsely because of some temporary sin. Now, there comes a point at which persistent error in the face of clear evidence to the contrary makes the possibility of false profession more likely than not. This is because the basic content of saving faith is repeated clearly in scripture numerous times, and would be regularly presented by any true church, with the result that continuing rejection of that faith could not plausibly be explained by ignorance. Rather, rejection in such cases will be better explained by a bad will, which as we saw above makes the difference between saving and dead faith, and which merits church discipline. But the principle of charity should lead us to assume a cause of ignorance before malice, and it's clear from experience than in many cases bad will is not likely. There are too many cases of obviously pious, humble believers who disagree with each other to rule out the possibility of this reality. Further, examination of scripture shows that some matters are not as clear as others. Obscurity of writing and reference, along with the multitude and plurality of texts which speak to various loci of doctrine, make error easily possible without a bad will bent on rejecting a known truth.

What About Christians in Sin, and Apostasy?

The New Testament speaks on many occasions of how believers should handle other Christians engaged in some kind of sin. A comprehensive survey is impossible, but we can note a few cases. Historically the earliest case is obviously Jesus' detailed instructions for how to deal with offending brothers in Matthew 18:15-18, with repeated calls to repentance made by increasing numbers of church members, concluding with a call to shun the recalcitrant. Another often discussed case is 1 Cor. 5. But we should note others. Titus 3:10-11 says: "As for a person who stirs up division, after warning him once and then twice, have nothing more to do with him, knowing that such a person is warped and sinful; he is self-condemned." James 5:19-20 urges its readers as follows: "My brothers, if anyone among you wanders from the truth and someone brings him back, let him know that whoever brings back a sinner from his wandering will save his soul from death and will cover a multitude of sins." Similarly, Jude writes (1:22-23): "have mercy on those who doubt; save others by snatching them out of the fire; to others show mercy with fear, hating even the garment stained by the flesh."

A common feature of these texts is the adequacy or proportionality of the response to the behaviour evidenced. The central issue once again seems to be the presence of a bad will. Before shunning comes a warning, expressing a hope that the sin is a result of temporary forgetfulness or weakness. With further persistence in sin comes more severe responses, culminating in having "nothing to do with" the person. Given the corporate logic made clear in the more detailed texts like Matt. 18 and 1 Cor. 5,[12] it seems most likely that the texts commending eventual shunning are primarily intended for application by the local body of believers as a whole, no doubt ultimately in refusal of the Lord's Supper, rather than private individuals *per se*.[13] The case of restoration already mentioned in 2 Corinthians shows that eventual repentance was not consid-

---

[12] See V. George Shillington, "Atonement Texture in 1 Corinthians 5.5," *JSNT* 71 (1998): 29-50, who convincingly demonstrates a concern for the purity of the corporate body is foregrounded in that text, contrary to some readings which see it as aimed at the restoration of the offender primarily.

[13] Thanks to Patrick Stefan in personal correspondence for this insight.

ered impossible, other texts like 2 Thess. 3:14-15 remind those doing the shunning: "Do not regard [the offender] as an enemy, but warn him as a brother," and the whole tenor of Christianity is about calling sinners to repentance; it therefore seems unlikely that an absolute refusal of communication is what is in view here.

Nevertheless, it is evident from scripture and from experience that sometimes members of the church abandon their faith. Even among magisterial Protestants, there has been no consensus on the question of whether salvation can be lost.[14] But from what we have demonstrated above, there is certainly no indication in scripture that salvation can be lost while saving faith is still present, and this is sufficient to maintain the truth of the Protestant theory.

What About Those Who Have Never Heard?

When one accepts a real distinction between the visible and invisible church, the possibility becomes real of saved people existing at a given moment outside the recognition of any or all visible local churches. From a different angle, the question about "those who have never heard" has arisen from early days in church history, and persists to the present. The theory presented above provides a careful way into the resolution of this problem.

We have seen that saving faith has in common a humble will towards God's revelation, but that the content of the faith can differ depending on what revelation has been given to a person at a particular time and place. The revelation given to Adam and Noah differs in content from that given through the apostles in the New Testa-

---

[14] E.g., the Lutherans and Wesleyans have argued that it can, while most of the Reformed have denied.

ment, though it does not contradict it. And various texts, including Hebrews 11, make clear that at least some people had saving faith prior to the call of Abraham. This opens up the possibility of individuals having saving Noahide faith at the same time as Abraham, without having heard of the patriarch. In this type of person, they would have "heard" what Noah did, but not what Abraham did, and yet would still be saved.

As history moves on, the question persists: could such people still exist at "this" moment? We know from cases like Josiah's restoration of the law and Jesus' criticism of Pharisaic oral tradition that the beliefs of a society can be corrupted through time, and that this is in fact a good reason to have written scriptures. Yet oral tradition is also not inherently incapable of passing on true information, so this tendency entails no absolute consequences. Nevertheless, by the time of the Psalms (e.g., 96:5), and certainly by Paul's time (Rom. 3:9-18, Eph. 2:12), it is clear that scripture regards the generality of the human race as lost. The apostle's reasoning for the necessity of missionaries also assumes this point (Rom. 10:13-14):

> for "Whoever will call on the name of the Lord will be saved." How then will they call on Him in whom they have not believed? How will they believe in Him whom they have not heard? And how will they hear without a preacher?

At the same time, the occasional example of repentant or believing Gentiles in the later OT narrative (e.g., Naaman the Syrian, Nebuchadnezzar, the Ninevites at Jonah's preaching) suggest that the general Psalmic and Pauline judgment probably assumed the possibility of rare exceptions. But exceptions they must be, given the generalizations. However many rare cases like these that might exist in the Gentile world outside of the reach of the gospel, there are not enough to undermine the necessity Paul proclaims for sending missionaries.

Bringing the question up to the present day, there are further complicating factors. Christianity is now the largest religion in the world numerically, and has been present in various forms across through globe throughout the centuries. The days are gone when the visible church was a small sect in the Roman empire. On the other hand, the Reformation reminds us that not every form of Christianity that has spread preserves saving faith intact, or at least not clearly, and the de-Christianization that has happened to various peoples at various points in history shows us that the knowledge of the gospel can be forgotten, making once reached areas into new mission fields. The result is that the call to proclaim the gospel is as needed as ever, but that we cannot rule out the possibility of a rare individual member of the invisible church in the midst of largely unbelieving populations.

What About Church Authority and Membership?

In our discussion of discipline we noted that justification by faith makes sacerdotalism impossible: if one is saved by faith as soon as there is faith, there is no room to make salvation contingent upon subsequent actions or rituals, even including baptism and the Lord's Supper administered by a priest or pastor. And if salvation includes membership in the invisible church, then neither can membership in the church be prevented or caused by such subsequent actions. Further, if judgments by church members can be mistaken, as is obviously the case, then those judgments cannot have intrinsic power to exclude people from the invisible church and salvation.

Recently, some evangelicals associated with 9Marks have attempted to defend an institutionalist Protestant ecclesiology. Joseph Minich has explored this project in greater depth through reviewing Jonathan Leeman's *Political Church*,[15] but we can make a few summary points here. First, in light of the above restrictions on the power of visible church members (whether individual or in groups, as elders or as not), church authority must be understood as fallible and declarative of God's judgment, rather than infallible and/or intrinsically creative of them. Second, at the same time, as human institutions, local churches have the same kind of human powers as all human institutions do, in subordination to natural and divine positive law. This includes the power to set rules about the common life of the members, such as when and where they will meet, who will lead the community, what kind of activities will happen in their meetings and outside them, and who will be included and excluded from them. Therefore, third, no Christian, individually or in community, has a right to knowingly exclude someone contrary to God's command that they be included. However, as long as they do not perceive a contradiction between their own judgment and God's, they are permitted and required to make fallible judgments of this nature. The well-being of the church

---

[15] See Joseph Minich, "Reviewing Jonathan Leeman's 'Political Church' Pt 1," *Mere Orthodoxy*, June 13, 2016, https://mereorthodoxy.com/reviewing-jonathan-leemans-political-church-pt-1/ and "Reviewing Jonathan Leeman's "Political Church" Pt. 2," *Mere Orthodoxy*, June 15, 2016, https://mereorthodoxy.com/reviewing-jonathan-leemans-political-church-pt-2/ (both accessed on May 25, 2017).

requires it, and fallibility alone is not a sufficient reason to forego making necessary judgments. Fourth, such judgments will take into account not just what Scripture says, but also the appropriate decisions and realities of the community, such as who has been given the office of elder, whether disciplined individuals have received previous warnings, and other relevant facts.

Another related practical question, raised by some 9Marks authors,[16] is whether members must make a covenant of membership with their local church. Once again a detailed discussion is impossible, but a few notes can be made. First, Protestant soteriology rules out the necessity of such a covenant for salvation. Second, it is important to be clear about the meaning of the term "covenant," in light of the overuse of the term. Most relevantly, as Gordon Hugenberger has noted, covenants as such include an oath, which itself is implicitly self-maledictory.[17] This means that in the formation of a covenant, a person at least implicitly asks for divine punishment to be imposed in the case that they break their promise. Third, there is no clear evidence in scripture that members of the apostolic church were bound by such an oath to remain in their local communities. Baptism, if it is an oath, is made to God (1 Pet. 3:21). Paul does say "we" are one body because we partake of the Lord's Supper (1 Cor. 10:17). Yet the practice of the Supper was universal, as was the referent of the "body of Christ" in the apostle's general use of the term. This

---

[16] E.g., Jonathan Leeman, *The Church and the Surprising Offense of God's Love: Reintroducing the Doctrines of Church Membership and Discipline* (Wheaton: Crossway Books, 2010).

[17] Gordon Paul Hugenberger, *Marriage as a Covenant* (Leiden: Brill, 1994), 168-215.

should incline us to understand Paul as saying the common practice of the church made it one body, and that this included members of local churches. The implied oath is also more naturally understood as directed towards the Lord, as in baptism. Fourth, as in the present day, so in the ancient world, there could be many morally licit reasons to change churches, such as business requiring a change of location. Fifth, then, the very real problem of church hopping and consumerism should not be opposed with an unfounded idea of membership covenants, but rather with an honest search into motives of heart. Individuals ought to only make changes in church communities if such are compatible with a real desire for the well-being of both communities, and with wisdom. It is certainly true that a general rootlessness through a community begets a lack of knowledge about the lives and hearts of its members, and this cannot be compatible with real love for them.

CONCLUSION

In his famous essay on the freedom of the Christian, Martin Luther summed up his message in his memorable aphorism: "A Christian man is the most free lord of all, and subject to none; a Christian man is the most dutiful servant of all, and subject to every one."[18] This also summarizes the argument of this chapter. By faith, a person is united to God, and his soul and fate are secured, beyond the power of any mere human to harm. Yet, that same faith generates love in that person for God and his creatures, which re-

---

[18] Martin Luther, "On the Freedom of a Christian," in *First Principles of the Reformation*, ed. Henry Wace and C. A. Buchheim (London: John Murray, 1883), 1998, http://sourcebooks.fordham.edu/halsall/mod/luther-freedomchristian.asp (accessed on May 25, 2017).

sults in words and actions that promote their good. The life of the visible church in its many forms flows from this one root. When we see this fact, we can understand everything God has said about the church, and everything that we know about it from experience, in sharp clarity. And this, in the end, is why all churches should adopt this Protestant ecclesiology: because it is manifestly true.

X:

PROTESTANT ECCLESIOLOGY AMONG CONTEMPORARY POLITICAL THEOLOGIES

Jake Meador

I DON'T THINK I'll ever forget the day that I actually began to understand some of what Reformed theology means on a day-to-day basis. I was a sophomore in college, living near campus in a small one-bedroom apartment by myself. One rainy evening I was sitting in my living room reading *Far as the Curse is Found* by Michael Williams. Williams was talking about the value of the physical creation to God, arguing that God isn't simply saving human souls or even human individuals, but will actually, one day, restore all of creation. It was something I hadn't heard before, having grown up in an old school dispensational church where it was simply a matter of common agreement that all of creation would one day be destroyed by God and, therefore, evangelism and Bible study was really all that mattered. "Only three things are eternal," we were told, "God, his Word, and human souls."

Williams' book was dismantling that idea in front of me in ways that both disoriented and delighted me. It disoriented me because it seemed to reject, explicitly or tacitly, so much of the theology I had known as a child. It delighted me because it meant that the delight I took in created things was, in fact, a good thing. Indeed, thanking God for those things and the joy they gave me was suddenly an act of worship rather than the simple indulgence of weakened flesh. As I finished the chapter, I put the book down, put a kettle of tea on the stove, and grabbed Ted Kooser's *Delights and Shadows* off my shelf. I had long been interested in poetry but had struggled to justify that love as a Christian. "Shouldn't you be reading the Bible or some devotional book instead?" people had asked me. I had asked myself the same question a time or two. But Williams was helping me to understand something about my love for poetry. And so I went out to the front porch to watch the spring rain. It seemed like the right thing to do.

THE PROBLEM OF THE CHURCH IN POLITICAL SOCIETY

The question of how the institutional church should relate to civil society is, of course, one of the oldest in Christian theology. In the contemporary West, a few separate schools have emerged. Several see the contemporary liberal order as being unsalvageable and thus in needs of some sort of fairly dramatic repudiation. Others want to work within the order to promote the common good, believing that the hyper-individualism we see today is no better or worse than any other way of organizing society.

Let's begin by defining what we mean by hyper-individualism. Then we will briefly sketch out the various schools before developing the magisterial Protestant approach at greater length. A hyper-individual social order sees each individual person as being a free, unattached, and self-defined whole. The true and just society is the society that allows or enables the maximal amount of freedom to each individual person. Consequently, hyper-individual social orders will generally be suspicious of institutions that claim to have some level of authority to bind individuals or curtail individual freedom. Part of this is epistemological in nature—we have lost faith in our ability to know things about the world and *especially* about morality, metaphysics, or the supernatural with any confidence. Thus public claims that are based in those disciplines are viewed with suspicion. This epistemological uncertainty also means that, so far they go, our ethical deliberations cannot really progress beyond the "do no harm" principle because we simply do not trust claims about things like a human individual's proper end, let alone the proper ends of human society.

The strength of liberalism is that it generally does resist most forms of social injustice or tyranny. The fierce individualism of the order causes its members to be sparked to action when something occurs which is seen as violating an individual person's right to freedom and self-definition. Even this strength can be overstated, of course, as one glance at the number of aborted babies since *Roe v Wade* will demonstrate. But it is true that as America has become more deeply liberal, it has also become less tolerant of a number of social evils— racism most particularly. And that is not an empty point.

That being said, the weaknesses of liberalism are many. T. S. Eliot made the point well in *The Idea of a Christian Society* when he said that liberal democracies are defined less by a fixed central point and more by a trajectory. Liberal democracies accumulate a great deal of energy and wealth, but then have no means for telling their members what to do with that wealth. They are centrifugal rather than centripetal. Thus we see the sort of social decline and breakdown lamented across the political spectrum today by thinkers like Bob Putnam[1] and George Packer[2] on the left and Rod Dreher[3] and Yuval Levin[4] on the right. Liberalism does not really have a strong mechanism for shaping social life, and so liberal orders tend to develop communal norms through a parasitical relationship with whatever order came before it in a given place.

SIX MODELS FOR THE CHURCH IN POLITICAL SOCIETY

With that introduction out of the way, we should review six distinct approaches to this question. We'll describe the first five briefly before developing the final version, magisterial Protestantism, in much more detail.

There are three distinct post-liberal strategies which all agree on one basic point: liberalism has failed. The first school, Roman Catholic Integralism, would follow the lead of traditional Roman political theology and argue that the just society is a society ordered toward its proper spiritual ends and thus is a society existing beneath the authority of

---

[1] Robert Putnam, *Our Kids: The American Dream in Crisis* (New York: Simon & Schuster, 2016).

[2] George Packer, *The Unwinding: An Inner History of the New America* (New York: Farrar, Straus and Giroux, 2013).

[3] Rod Dreher, *The Benedict Option: A Strategy for Christians in a Post-Christian Nation* (New York: Sentinel, 2017).

[4] Yuval Levin, *Fractured Republic: Renewing America's Social Contract in the Age of Individualism* (New York: Basic Books, 2016).

the Roman church, which is the instrument by which people can realize their proper spiritual end[5].

The second school, Radical Anabaptism, descends from the 16th century Radical Reformation and embraces a strict biblicism, a simple lifestyle, some form of Christian non-violence, and often some kind of shared living arrangement which sometimes goes so far as renouncing all forms of private property. For radical Anabaptists, to borrow from their preeminent theologian Stanley Hauerwas, "The church does not have a social ethic; the church is a social ethic."[6] The church is the true and complete society and so we commit our lives fully to the building up of *that* society. We are only involved in society outside of the church to the extent that necessity requires us to be.

The third post-liberal school is post-liberal retreatists. This category is something of a catch-all for Protestant Christians who basically share the Radical Anabaptist critique of civil society and perhaps even aspects of Radical Anabaptist ecclesiology, but do not embrace other aspects of their theology, such as their biblicism, non-violence, or denunciation of private property. For the post-liberal retreatists, the church might not be a complete society unto itself, but it is the safe society we have today and it is the refuge out of which the new post-liberal order will emerge. Thus we must commit ourselves to its life and well-being and mostly scale back our ambitions for society outside the church. If we must participate in that society, then we are

---

[5] The primary group working on the Integralist project at the moment is *The Josias*, a collective of writers led by *First Things* assistant editor Elliot Milco.

[6] Stanley Hauerwas, *The Peaceable Kingdom* (South Bend: University of Notre Dame Press, 1991).

best off to do so in purely defensive ways that will carve out as much freedom for Christians as possible so that we can better ride out the storm. Dreher's *Benedict Option* likely belongs to this school, as does the work of Ethics and Religious Liberty Commission President Russell Moore.

In addition to these three systems, there are two systems which hope to retain aspects of liberalism. These two groups are the Protestant individualists and Revanchist Individualists. These two groups are similar in many ways. They both affirm or, at least, accept hyper-individualism as a social order, valuing the freedom it affords from previous oppressive regimes. Where they drift apart is, for the most part, generational. The older members of this group tend toward revanchism, which is to say they think that the West has lost its way in recent years, but that we can and should take back the ground we lost and embrace a civil society that basically affirms the core tenets of liberalism, perhaps with a few slight handbrakes included to ward off the most pernicious forms of liberal self-expression. Old Religious Right leaders would belong to this group, as do some older American Catholics like George Weigel. The Protestant Individualists are younger and generally are more comfortable with the current order as is, provided said order does not become much more hostile to religious faith than it already is. For Protestant individualists, the current order is mostly a good and healthy thing which protects individual rights by weakening the social institutions that can cruelly and unjustly abuse individual people. The responsibility for Christians, then, is to participate in the existing institutions of civil society on all levels, working for the good of all people by strengthening the institutions that shape our social life.[7]

THE MAGISTERIAL PROTESTANTS ON THE CHURCH IN POLITICAL SOCIETY

The final school, which we will now spend the remainder of this essay discussing, is the Magisterial Protestant answer. For the Magisterial Protestants, none of these schools get the answer quite right, although the Catholic Integralists come the closest. Magisterial Protestant political theology and ecclesiology begins with a simple idea: there are two separate governments or realms by which Christ mediates his rule over his people and over creation. Significantly, however, these realms are not "church" and "state" or the "public" and "private" spheres. The answer is more complicated than that and does not neatly map onto contemporary debates about the role of religion in public life.

The two kingdoms of the Magisterial Protestant school are the temporal or visible kingdom and the spiritual kingdom[8]. If we are to understand how Magisterial Protestants relate church to society, we must understand this distinction rightly. In order to do that, we need to trace the distinction back to one of the core ideas of the Reformation: *sola fide*. When Luther said that man was justified by faith alone, his opponents were quick to accuse him of essentially destroying moral order. If our works

---

[7] I have written in more detail on each of these approaches at Mere Orthodoxy, which you can read more about here: https://mereorthodoxy.com/benedict-option-political-theology/.

[8] Brad Littlejohn, *The Two Kingdoms: A Guide for the Perplexed* (Moscow, ID: The Davenant Press: 2017).

have *nothing* to do with our salvation, why should we do good? Luther responded with his famous claim in *The Freedom of the Christian* that, "[a] Christian man is the most free lord of all, and subject to none; a Christian man is the most dutiful servant of all, and subject to every one." What is often missed by readers is how this teaching relates to social order. For Luther the two halves of that statement lay quite neatly atop the two realms he articulated elsewhere. In the spiritual realm, man stands before the face of God and, by faith, is justified. "Christ reigns mysteriously and invisibly over the kingdom of conscience, and no human authority may dare to interpose itself as the mediator of this rule."[9] The temporal kingdom, in contrast, is the realm in which the Christian is a servant to all as a member of the Christian commonwealth and as a person called to love his neighbor as Christ has loved him. This realm covers all human institutions, including individual local Christian congregations and denominational institutions.

The trouble many of us have in understanding this idea is that there is a natural inclination here to ask, "So if membership in the church has nothing to do with our justification, then what is the church for?" When we try to answer that question, there is a desire to sneak some sort of Romanism in through the back door. So you might hear congregationalists talking about the institutional church as an embassy for the Kingdom to come or Anabaptist radicals talking about the church being a *polis*. But these are simply muted versions of the same Roman error which elevates the institutional church to a place it was never intended to fill—as the center of the Christian life and a pivotal agent in the salvation of souls. But this cannot be

---

[9] Littlejohn, 15.

the case—Christ is the center. The institutional church is one means, the foremost amongst many others, for helping to further his work in creation. It is a unique means in that, as the institution entrusted to preach the Gospel, it is, one might say, *closer* to the invisible kingdom because we participate in it by virtue of our claim to spiritual membership, but *qua* institution, it is still part of the visible kingdom.

THREE KEYS TO THE MAGISTERIAL PROTESTANT VISION

There are three ideas which follow from this basic insight into the true nature of the institutional church.

First, the institutional church once again becomes apostolic in the original sense of the term—being "sent out." The church does not simply gather Christians into its bosom and shelter them from the storm nor does it somehow elevate those who belong to it toward a higher order of existence. The church largely exists to send people out into the world. Here, reflection on the traditional three marks of the church as defined by the Reformed tradition can be of help. The institutional church is defined by three traits: the preaching of the Gospel, the administration of the sacraments, and the practice of church discipline. Rightly understood, all three of these marks serve the purpose of equipping the saints to be sent out into the world to witness to the love and grace of God as they go about their daily lives. The thought of 16th century reformer Martin Bucer is especially instructive on this point. Bucer saw an intimate relationship between Christian love and Christian discipline.[10] We might even paraphrase John Piper's famous line, "Missions exist because worship does not," and say that, for Bucer, discipline exists because love does not. The purpose of Christian discipline is to help shape us in such a way that we are capable of living in Christian love with our neighbors both inside and outside of Christ's covenant community. Church discipline thus becomes simply an institutionalized form of Christian discipline to be used in emergency situations, as it were. Moreover, our reflection on the sacraments and particularly the Eucharist might be enriched by a closer attentiveness to the missional nature of the meal. The Reformed tradition generally has held that the Supper is not simply a memorial, but that there is some real sense in which it unites us to Christ. Because he is spiritually present in the Supper, we are united to him. Indeed, you may even reverse the normal way we tend to think of movement happening in the Supper. Rather than Christ coming down to us, we are caught up with him in a foreshadowing of the world to come where we partake with him of the Supper of the Lamb.[11] Having feasted with him, we are then sent out, strengthened, at the close of public worship in order to witness to the glory of God amongst our neighbors.

Second, the other institutions of the temporal realm take on new significance. While the institutional church

---

[10] Meador, Jake. "That No One Should Live for Himself, but for Others: Martin Bucer and the Third Mark of the Church," in W. Bradford Littlejohn and Jonathan Tomes, eds., *Beyond Calvin: Essays on the Diversity of the Reformed Tradition* (Moscow, ID: The Davenant Press, 2017).

[11] On the Reformed doctrine of the Lord's Supper, see Herman Bavinck, *Reformed Dogmatics* (Grand Rapids: Baker Academic, 2008), 4:540-85, and Michael Horton, *People and Place: A Covenant Ecclesiology* (Louisville: Westminster John Knox Press, 2008), 124-52.

has been entrusted with the preaching of the Word and the Sacraments, which does in some sense give it greater significance, it is still part of the visible kingdom and thus exists alongside the other institutions and work to be done in the commonwealth. It has a role to play in the Christian commonwealth, but so too do other institutions. This means that our work matters, not simply because it provides an income to support us and our families, but because it is a means by which we fulfill the divine command to fill and subdue creation. Likewise, vocation matters. The unique callings we are given carry enormous significance and should not be deemed as being less valuable simply because they are not formal, full-time ministry work. These realms become practical ways of showing love to neighbor and, by extension, love to God. In other words, there is no sacred/secular split in the way this term is often used.

Third, we recover the idea of the Christian *commonwealth* rather than a sort of hierarchically structured society existing under the church or a secular society in which freedom of religion is respected, thereby leaving "a place" for the church (but little more than that). This is a central idea in the history of Reformed thought. Indeed, the legacy of this idea can be found in the official names of several American states, such as the Commonwealth of Virginia. Briefly stated, the idea is that human beings are inextricably social and so human societies must be understood as a shared enterprise amongst all the members of a community. Moreover, because all the institutions that shape society are part of the visible rather than the spiritual kingdom, society should not be understood as a hierarchical structure in which the church sits atop the rest of the social institutions. Rather, social power is diffused across a variety of different institutions and groups. There are roles within a society properly given to the institutional church, but also roles properly ascribed to the family, to schools, to the market, and to the magistrate. All these different social bodies together comprise the Christian commonwealth.

This idea of a Christian commonwealth, which clearly is not the same thing as an ecclesiocracy (as you might have in Roman Catholic states or even in Puritan New England), is a difficult thing to convey since the entire notion of a Christian commonwealth has been forgotten not only in the contemporary American republic generally, but even within much evangelical reflection on social order. This is not surprising—the notion of a Christian commonwealth is by definition a pervasive criticism of the way American social order is often defined and discussed. The American liberal order rests largely on the assumption that human beings are essentially private, self-enclosed individuals. At his most basic level, man is solitary. Thus the system of government exists to facilitate and enable that individual freedom as we have already said. But it also rests on an assumption that man is not an intrinsically political creature given to societies and communities he has not chosen. This, of course, is nonsensical. We are all born into a multitude of communities which we have not chosen but which will, nevertheless, do a great deal to shape and define who we are as individual people. A political system which fails to reckon with this fact will prove to be brittle and unsustainable, as we are seeing quite clearly in the contemporary United States. Understanding society not as a group of individuals knit together by a tacit social contract, but instead as people belonging to a shared commonwealth, helps us to understand concepts like solidarity more clearly—as well as why specific Christian teachings work in the way that they do. For example, Christian sexual ethics make far more sense if man is a rooted member of a commonwealth than they do if he is a detached and autonomous individual.

The relevance of this point in particular to contemporary American political disputes should be abundantly clear to anyone who pays a passing attention to the circus-like atmosphere that prevails in our nation's politics. As the recent election of Donald Trump made plain, there is a large portion of our nation's electorate which, whatever else you might say about them, desperately longs for someone in power to stand with them. The typical Trump voter supported President Trump not least because he believed, almost certainly falsely, that Trump would represent him and his interests in Washington. This is why so many of the people who flocked to Washington for Trump's inauguration spoke of how they'd never been to Washington before. Trump was tapping into something real, a felt longing amongst a certain class of Americans to be *seen*. Of course, on the other side of the spectrum there is a similar sort of fear we might call solidarity anxiety: Consider the underlying fear that explains movements like Black Lives Matter. The fear for African Americans is that they will do everything America tells them to do and it won't matter. They will *still* not belong, still will not be treated as a normal member of the American republic. The same concern drives a great deal of the activism from pro-LGBT activists. One friend of mine framed the debate about bathrooms and transgenderism as a debate about a person's right to exist in public. You can (and should) disagree with that assessment of the debate, but the framing is suggestive. Once again, the longing is to be seen and recognized as one actually is. The irony, of course, is that in matters of sexual ethics in particular, we demand both the freedom to define ourselves however we wish *and* that society recognize whatever identity we land on—regardless of the costs to society entailed in such an act. It is incoherent, but in a way that tells us something about the base difficulty with liberalism. There is, in our deeply individualistic society, an undeniable longing for solidarity, for communal membership and recognition—for roots. A Christian political theology will recognize this longing and identify it as a function of living in a state that functionally denies those needs.

The magisterial Protestant vision of a Christian commonwealth is particularly equipped to do this work for the simple reason that belonging and social capital are diffused more broadly than they are in other social orders precisely *because* single earthly institutions are not privileged over others in such a way that the laity are second-class citizens or that one loses all rights as a citizen if one is under church discipline. The institutional church does not control social capital, nor does a small Christian community become a social body unto itself, removed from broader civil society. The magisterial Protestant approach sees a missional church integrated into the basic structure of a society, equipping people to love and serve their neighbors. This focus on outreach and the common good, as well as the proper placement of the institutional church relative to civil society, should all help to mitigate against totalitarian tendencies that could emerge in a movement.

THE GOODNESS OF ALL VOCATIONS

Here we might return to that experience I had during a spring storm while reading *Far as the Curse is Found*. The reason I smiled, made some tea, and then sat on the porch to read some poetry is simple: As I began to understand what the Reformed tradition teaches, I realized that my work as a student was valuable in itself. The university where I was studying was not simply a convenient tool for rounding up all the godless youths into a single place to facilitate easier evangelistic outreach, as many campus ministries seem to believe on a functional level. Studying literature and history (I was an English and History major) were worthwhile pursuits in themselves. In studying these subjects, I was learning about wisdom and virtue and politics and beauty and a host of other things which make life worth living and help communities live well together. This work was good because it equipped me to be a better neighbor, citizen, and churchmen and so it was work that God smiled upon. These interests of mine, then, were not simply personal proclivities that might be made into a career, as many of my peers in these programs believed, but were actually intimately related to the work God had given me to do in the place where he had put me. What better way to celebrate such a realization then by watching a spring storm and thanking God for the rain while reading a magical description of the storm like this? "I sat in the cellar / from six to eight while fat spring clouds / went somersaulting, rumbling east. Then it poured, / a storm that walked on legs of lightning, / dragging its shaggy belly over the fields."[12] That image, playing out before my eyes as I watched the storms roll in helped me see God's creation more clearly and to delight in the goodness of God all the more.

Critics of the magisterial tradition might charge that it so dramatically curtails the power of the institutional church that the church loses its significance as a social body. But the reality is quite the opposite: It elevates the life of the commonwealth such that *every* honorable vocation is now glorious and worthy of pursuit. It makes accessible to all people the contentment and sense of eternal purpose in one's work that the western church has far too often limited to only ministers and missionaries. Magisterial Protestant ecclesiology does not diminish the church; it exalts the commonwealth.

Therefore, in closing, we return to Luther: A Christian man is the most free lord of all, and subject to none; a Christian man is the most dutiful servant of all, and subject to everyone. The first step in building a Christian commonwealth is a simple one: We look for opportunities to serve the places in which we live by promoting common life and, when questioned as to *why* we serve in these ways, "giving an account of the hope that is within us." Such a payoff may perhaps seem too modest: "So you're telling me that the first step toward social transformation is volunteering with a refugee resettlement group, starting a business to provide employment for local people, or leading a Bible study at the homeless shelter? That seems… small?" Answer: It is small. But we serve a King whose kingdom, by his own admission, is upside down, who tells

[12] Ted Kooser, "Mother," http://writersalmanac.publicradio.org/index.php?date=2011/04/29 (accessed on July 3, 2017).

us that the first shall be last and the last first. The first step to cultivating a Christian commonwealth is becoming a more thoroughly Christian citizen. And the first step toward *that* is serving faithfully in the "small" matters of life.

XI:
CONCLUSION

Joseph Minich

EVERY week, Christians confess together, "We believe in one, holy, catholic, and apostolic, church." One way of summing up the argument of this book is that the Protestant doctrine of the church is implicit in the creed that Christians always already find themselves confessing—precisely because that creed is grounded in reality. Taking each element of this ancient phrase, note that the church is ultimately an article of faith. Its essence is not visible in the way that it will be at the last day. The church is marked visibly by word and sacrament, but its visible expression does not map exactly or neatly onto the spiritual reality. Its visible expression and spiritual essence will be perfectly suited to one another in the new heavens and earth—but the difficult work of earthly ecclesiology is to understand this relationship while we wait for this glorious day. Some disciplinarian ecclesiologies are self-consciously motivated to make that correspondence as close as possible by the rigorous removal of sinners. Sacerdotal ecclesiologies more or less conflate the visible with the invisible churches, but as we have seen, have to adjust this a bit to account for reality itself. In our judgment, recognizing this tension (which just is a tension in reality) is the genius of Protestant ecclesiology. We do not adjust our primary ecclesiological axioms like a Procrustean bed to "account for" these tensions. Rather, these are founding axioms, and discipline, the role of clergy (etc.) are mapped onto these fundamental realities of life in anticipation of glory—as guided by Holy Scripture. And fascinatingly, with Scripture as our guide, it must be noted that the New Testament is far less concerned with "exact overlap" between the two realms as we are. Suited precisely to the fallen world in which we find ourselves, the New Testament speaks in precisely the ways that objections to Protestant ecclesiology might foreclose. Let us note this by looking at the rest of the Creed's description of the church.

The unity of the church is both an already (Eph. 4:4) and a not yet (Eph. 4:13). The holiness of the church is both an already (Eph. 1:1-5) and a not yet (Eph. 5:26). The Catholicity of the church is both an already (Eph. 4:4) and a not yet (Rev. 5—including the whole earth!). Even the apostolicity of the church is ultimately its grounding in a word, the calling of which it still pursues and seeks to attain (Eph. 4:11-13). Indeed, Paul himself does not claim any innate authority over his message, but precisely the reverse. He tells the Galatians that they ought to condemn him (and even an angel!) if he ever proclaimed to them a different word than the one he already delivered (Gal. 6:1-10). It is remarkable to note that he expects that his Galatian audience ought to be able to discern even if an apostle went astray from the Word (as Peter in Gal. 2:11, for instance). The New Testament navigates the tension between the two ages with tremendous realism. Indeed, I would wager that any objection to Protestant ecclesiology's groundedness in reality could be converted into an objection to the church in the New Testament. Should not the visible church's relationship to the invisible church be preserved by a requirement of maximal holiness and unity and universality? It would be hard to square this with Paul's epistles to the Corinthian church. Certainly there are cases of excommunication in the Corinthian correspondence, but it is worth noting the extent to which Paul takes a very pastoral posture toward scandal—and apparently over many years. The people of Corinth struggle with unity as much as any American evangelical church. They struggle with holiness as much as any American evangelical church. They struggle with catholicity as much as any American evangelical church (2 Corinthians 8 encourages them to communal participation with others). Indeed, they struggle with apostolicity as much as any American evangelical church (whether the apostolic message of the resurrection in 1 Corinthians, or the apostle himself in 2 Corinthians!).

In my judgment, these dynamics are the objects of many ecclesiological complaints. How does the apostle evaluate these dynamics? Confidence and boasting (2 Cor. 2:3 and 7:4)! Wherever vestiges of the word and of the gospel remain (despite disunity, despite worldliness, despite insularity, despite a distorted relation to the apostle), there remains the earth-shattering power of almighty God who announces justice to sinners and whose word ripples through their lives and communities like the epicenter of an earthquake the heals the world rather than fragments it. And let it be noted: this is to the glory of God. To wish for a less messy ecclesiology is perhaps to unwittingly rob God of His honor. It is precisely to the glory of His grace that His people and His church are just like this—at the same time just and sinful—free from all but the servants of all. We will know that we see with the eyes and the heart of God when we could look at a church like that of Corinth and say, "Great is my boasting on your behalf."

But we are not done with the Creed. Attentive readers might note that I have passed over the word, "we." To speak collectively with this "we," joining our voice to a chorus of confessors, is precisely to be caught up in a movement of the Spirit which has not yet finished. The partial reversal of Babel in Acts 2 will become its utter eradication in the healing of the nations which we find in Revelation 22. The "we" who find themselves in-between these poles are called to particulate and cultivate that movement of the Spirit to which they belong. All authority in heaven and on earth has been given to Christ, and He has called the church (as a redeemed inflection of the original commission given to Adam) to participate in that healing of the nations through the gospel which is finished in Revelation 22 (Mat. 28:16-20). I suspect that we cannot have Paul's perspective about the Corinthians without this narrative framework. The church can be messed up, but Christ is with it through His spirit. And whatever it might seem like, He is at work perfecting and growing it. And here we find ourselves, twenty-first century American evangelicals. We are just like the Corinthians in many ways. But despite these sinful instruments, the church has grown. The forgiveness of sins has been proclaimed. The love of Christ has been shared. Let us boast.

XII.

BIBLIOGRAPHY

Joseph Minich: The Church Question in a Disoriented Age

Allen, Michael, and Scott Swain. *Reformed Catholicity: The Promise of Retrieval for Theology and Biblical Interpretation.* Grand Rapids: Baker Academic, 2015.

Berman, Marshall. *All That is Solid Melts Into Air: The Experience of Modernity.* New York: Penguin, 1982.

Bauman, Zygmund. *Liquid Modernity.* New York: Polity, 2000.

Gregory, Brad. *The Unintended Reformation: How a Religious Revolution Secularized Society.* Cambridge: Harvard University Press, 2012.

Leeman, Jonathan. *The Church and the Surprising Offense of God's Love: Reintroducing the Doctrines of Church Membership and Discipline.* Wheaton: Crossway, 2009.

—. *Political Church: The Local Assembly as Embassy of Christ's Rule.* Downers Grove: InterVarsity Press, 2016.

Popkin, Richard. *The History of Skepticism: From Savonarola to Bayle.* New York: Oxford University Press, 2003.

Rodgers, Daniel. *Age of Fracture.* Cambridge: Harvard University Press, 2011.

Van Drunen, David. *Living in God's Two Kingdoms: A Biblical Vision for Christianity and Culture*. Wheaton: Crossway, 2010.

Bradley Belschner: The Protestant Doctrine of the Church and its Rivals

Bavinck, Hermann. *Reformed Dogmatics*. Grand Rapids: Baker House Company, 2008.

Boniface VIII. "Unam Sanctam: One God, One Faith, One Spiritual Authority." *Papal Encyclicals Online*. Accessed on August 15, 2016.
http://www.papalencyclicals.net/Bon08/B8unam.htm.

Cyril. *Lettres Anecdotes de Cyrille Lucar*. Amsterdam: Chez L'Honore et Chatelain, 1718.

"Fifth Lateran Council." *Legion of Mary -Tidewater, Virginia*. Accessed on August 15, 2016.
http://www.legionofmarytidewater.com/faith/ECUM18.HTM.

Hadjiantoniou, George A. *Protestant Patriarch: The Life of Cyril Lucaris, 1572-1638*. Richmond, VA: John Knox Press, 1961.

Leo X. "Exsurge Domine." *Papal Encyclicals Online*. Accessed on August 15, 2016.
http://www.papalencyclicals.net/Leo10/l10exdom.htm.

Lowrie, Walter. *The Church & Its Organization in Primitive & Catholic Times: An Interpretation of Rudolph Sohm's Kirchenrecht*. Longmans: New York, 1904.

Oberman, Heiko. *Luther: Man Between God and the Devil*. New Haven: Yale University Press, 1989.

Pink, Thomas. "What is the Catholic doctrine of religious liberty?" Accessed on September 8, 2016. https://www.academia.edu/639061/What_is_the_Catholic_doctrine_of_religious_liberty.

"Second Helvetic Confession." *Christian Classics Ethereal Library*. Accessed on August 15, 2016. https://www.ccel.org/creeds/helvetic.htm.

Stewart, Alistair. *The Original Bishops*. Grand Rapids: Baker Academic, 2014.

Tertullian. *De Exhortatione Castitatis*. In *Fathers of the Third Century: Tertullian, Part Fourth; Minucius Felix; Commodian; Origen, Parts First and Second*, vol. 4 of *The Ante-Nicene Church Fathers*. Buffalo, NY: Christian Literature Publishing, 1885.

Weber, F. Alexander. *The Moral Argument Against War in Eastern Orthodox Theology*. San Francisco: International Scholars Publications, 1998.

"Westminster Confession of Faith." *Center for Reformed Theology and Apologetics*. Accessed on August 15, 2016. http://www.reformed.org/documents/westminster_conf_of_faith.html.

Wynn, Phillip. *Augustine on War and Military Service*. Minneapolis: Fortress Press, 2013.

Steven Wedgeworth: Finding Zion: The Church in the Old Testament

Bannerman, D. Douglas. *The Scripture Doctrine of the Church Historically and Exegetically Considered*. Edinburgh: T&T Clark, 1887.

Barker, Margaret. *Heaven on Earth*. Edited by T. Desmond Alexander and Simon Gathercole. Carlisle: Paternoster, 2004.

—. *The Gate of Heaven*. Sheffield: Sheffield Phoenix Press, 2008.

—. *Temple Theology: An Introduction*. London: SPCK, 2004.

Bavinck, Herman. *Reformed Dogmatics*. Grand Rapids: Baker Academic, 2008.

Burtchaell, James Tunstead. *From Synagogue to Church*. Cambridge: Cambridge University Press, 1992.

Calvin, John. *Institutes of the Christian Religion* Translated by Ford Lewis Battles and edited by John McNeill. Louisville, KY: Westminster Press, 1960.

Dunn, James D.G. *Jesus Remembered*. Grand Rapids: William B. Eerdmans, 2013.

Leithart, Peter J. *From Silence to Song: The Davidic Liturgical Revolution*. Moscow, ID: Canon Press, 2003.

Lowrie, Walter. *The Church and Its Organization In Primitive and Catholic Times*. New York: Longmans, Green, and Co, 1904.

Trigg, Jonathan D. *Baptism in the Theology of Martin Luther*. Leiden: Brill, 1994.

E.J. Hutchinson, Excursus: What is the "Church"? Etymology and Concept in Classical Antiquity, the LXX, and the New Testament

F.H. Jacobson, "Church, The Christian." In Samuel Macauley Jackson (ed.), *The New Schaff-Herzog Encyclopedia of Religious Knowledge*, vol. 3, 77-85. Grand Rapids, MI: Baker, 1952.

Alastair Roberts: Pentecost as Ecclesiology

Heschel, Joshua. *Heavenly Torah: As Refracted Through the Generations*. Edited and translated by Gordon Tucker. London: Continuum, 2006.

Park, Sejin. *Pentecost and Sinai: The Festival of Weeks as a Celebration of the Sinai Event*. London: T & T Clark, 2008.

Roberts, Alastair. "Infant Baptism and the Promise of Grace." *Reformation21.org*. Accessed on September 27, 2016. http://www.reformation21.org/articles/infant-baptism-and-the-when-of-baptismal-grace.php.

"The Politics of the King's Donkey." *Political Theology.com*. Accessed on September 27, 2016. http://www.politicaltheology.com/blog/the-politics-of-the-kings-donkey-luke-1928-40/.

Bradford Littlejohn: *Simul Justus et Peccator*: The Genius and Tensions of Reformation Ecclesiology

Avis, Paul D.L. *The Church in the Theology of the Reformers*. London: Marshall, Morgan, and Scott, 1981.

Avis, Paul D.L. "The True Church in Reformation Theology." *Scottish Journal of Theology* 30, no. 4 (1977): 319-345.

Ballor, Jordan J., and Littlejohn, W. Bradford. "European Calvinism: Church Discipline." In Irene Dingel and Johannes Paulmann, eds., *European History Online* (EGO). Mainz: Institute of European History (IEG), 2013, http://www.ieg-ego.eu/en/threads/crossroads/religious-and-denominational-spaces/jordan-ballor-w-bradford-littlejohn-european-calvinism-church-discipline.

Brachlow, Stephen. *The Communion of Saints: Radical Puritan and Separatist Ecclesiology, 1570–1625*. Oxford: Oxford University Press, 1988.

Collinson, Patrick. *The Elizabethan Puritan Movement*. Oxford: Clarendon, 1967.

—. *The Religion of Protestants: The Church in English Society, 1559–1625*. Oxford: Clarendon Press, 1982.

D. Martin Luther's Werke: kritische Gesamtausgabe (Weimarer Ausgabe). 120 vols. Weimar: H. Böhlaus Nachfolger, 1883–2009.

Davis, Kenneth R. "No Discipline, No Church: An Anabaptist Contribution to the Reformed Tradition." *The Sixteenth Century Journal* 13, no. 4 (1982): 43-58.

Estes, James M. *Peace, Order, and the Glory of God: Secular Authority and the Church in the Thought of Luther and Melanchthon, 1518–1559*. Leiden: Brill, 2005.

Fincham, Kenneth. *Prelate as Pastor: The Episcopate of James I*. Oxford: Clarendon Press, 1990.

Lewis, Gillian. "Calvinism in Geneva in the Time of Calvin and Beza (1541–1605)." In Menna Prestwich, ed., *International Calvinism, 1541–1715*. Oxford: Clarendon Press, 1985.

Littlejohn, W. Bradford. *Richard Hooker: A Companion to His Life and Work*. Eugene, OR: Cascade, 2015.

Luther, Martin. *Three Treatises, from the American Edition of Luther's Works*. Minneapolis: Fortress Press, 1966.

Meador, Jake. "'That No One Should Live for Himself, but for Others': Love and the Third Mark of the Church in the Theology of Martin Bucer." In W. Bradford Littlejohn and Jonathan Tomes, ed., *Beyond Calvin: Essays on the Diversity of the Reformed Tradition*. Moscow, ID: The Davenant Press, 2017.

Nevin, John Williamson. "The Sect System, Article 1." *Mercersburg Review* 1, no. 5 (1849): 482-507.

Pelikan, Jaroslav, and Helmut T. Lehmann, eds. *Luther's Works: American Edition*. St. Louis: Concordia Publishing House, and Philadelphia: Muhlenberg Press, 1955–1970.

Springer, Michael. *Restoring Christ's Church: John á Lasco and the Forma Ac Ratio*. Aldershot: Ashgate, 2007.

Sykes, Norman. *Old Priest and New Presbyter*. Cambridge: CUP, 1957.

Tuininga, Matthew. *Calvin's Political Theology and the Public Engagement of the Church: Christ's Two Kingdoms*. Cambridge: CUP, 2017.

Winship, Michael P. *Godly Republicanism: Puritans, Pilgrims, and a City on a Hill*. Cambridge, MA: Harvard University Press, 2012.

Andre A. Gazal: English Reformation: "A Heavenly Office, A Holy Ministry": Ordination in the English Reformation

Book of Common Prayer. Oxford: Oxford University Press, 1969.

Gazal, Andre A. *Scripture and Royal Supremacy in Tudor England: The Use of Old Testament Historical Narrative*. Lewiston, NY: Edwin Mellen, Press, 2013.

Jewel, John. *Apology of the Church of England*. Translated by Ann Bacon, and edited by John Booty. New York: Church Publishing, 2002.

—. *The Works of John Jewel*. Edited by John Ayre. 4 vols. Cambridge: The University Press, 1845-50.

Pelikan, Jaroslav. *The Growth of Medieval Theology (600–1300)*. Chicago: University of Chicago Press, 1978.

Jones, Norman. *Faith By Statute, Parliament and the Settlement of Religion, 1559*. London: Royal Historical Society, 1982.

Jordan Ballor: Excursus: Church Discipline as a Way of Love

Hauerwas, Stanley, "Christianity: It's Not a Religion, It's an Adventure." In John Berkman and Michael Cartwright, eds., *The Hauerwas Reader*, 522–38. Durham: Duke University Press, 2001.

—. "Abortion, Theologically Understood." In Berkman and Cartwright, eds, *The Hauerwas Reader*, 603–22.

"Teaching of the Twelve Apostles." In Canon Spence, trans., *The Teaching of the Twelve Apostles*. London: James Nisbet & Co., 1885.

Wells, David F., *God in the Wasteland: The Reality of Truth in a World of Fading Dreams*. Grand Rapids: Eerdmans, 1994).

Andrew Fulford: Protestant Ecclesiology as Good Theory

Bavinck, Herman. *Reformed Dogmatics*. Translated by John Vriend, and ed. John Bolt. Grand Rapids: Baker Academic, 2008.

Carson, D.A. "Matthew." In *Matthew and Mark*, ed. David E. Garland and Tremper Longman, III. Revised ed. Vol. 9 of *The Expositor's Bible Commentary*. Grand Rapids: Zondervan, 2010.

Ciampa, Roy E., and Brian S. Rosner. *The First Letter to the Corinthians.* The Pillar New Testament Commentary. Grand Rapids: Wm. B. Eerdmans, 2010.

Ferguson, Everett. *Baptism in the Early Church.* Grand Rapids: Wm. B. Eerdmans, 2009.

Hooker, Richard. *A learned and comfortable sermon of the certaintie and perpetuitie of faith in the elect especially of the prophet Habakkuks faith.* 2nd ed. Oxford: Joseph Barnes, 1612.

Hugenberger, Gordon Paul. *Marriage as a Covenant.* Leiden: Brill, 1994.

Leeman, Jonathan. *The Church and the Surprising Offense of God's Love: Reintroducing the Doctrines of Church Membership and Discipline.* Wheaton: Crossway Books, 2010.

Luther, Martin. "On the Freedom of a Christian." In *First Principles of the Reformation.* Edited by Henry Wace and C. A. Buchheim. London: John Murray, 1883. Accessed on May 25, 2017. http://sourcebooks.fordham.edu/halsall/mod/luther-freedomchristian.asp.

Muller, Richard A. *The Unaccommodated Calvin* (New York: Oxford University, 2000), 170.

New American Standard Bible. La Habra: Foundation Press, 1995.

Perks, Stephen C. *The Christian Passover: Agape Feast or Ritual Abuse?.* Taunton: Kuyper Foundation, 2012.

Shillington, V. George. "Atonement Texture in 1 Corinthians 5.5." *JSNT* 71 (1998): 29-50.

Wright, N.T. *Acts, Romans, 1 Corinthians*, vol. 10 of *The New Interpreter's Bible.* Nashville: Abingdon Press.

Jake Meador: Protestant Ecclesiology Among Contemporary Political Theologies

Bavinck, Herman. *Reformed Dogmatics*. Grand Rapids: Baker Academic, 2008.

Dreher, Rod. *The Benedict Option: A Strategy for Christians in a Post-Christian Nation*. New York: Sentinel, 2017.

Hauerwas, Stanley. *The Peaceable Kingdom*. South Bend: University of Notre Dame Press, 1991.

Kooser, Ted. "Mother." Accessed on July 3, 2017. http://writersalmanac.publicradio.org/index.php?date=2011/04/29.

Levin, Yuval. *Fractured Republic: Renewing America's Social Contract in the Age of Individualism*. New York: Basic Books, 2016.

Littlejohn, W. Bradford. *The Two Kingdoms: A Guide for the Perplexed*. Moscow, ID: Davenant Press: 2017.

Meador, Jake. "That No One Should Live for Himself, but for Others: Martin Bucer and the Third Mark of the Church." In W. Bradford Littlejohn and Jonathan Tomes, eds. *Beyond Calvin: Essays on the Diversity of the Reformed Tradition*. Moscow, ID: Davenant Press, 2017.

Packer, George. *The Unwinding: An Inner History of the New America*. New York: Farrar, Straus and Giroux, 2013.

Putnam, Robert. *Our Kids: The American Dream in Crisis*. New York: Simon & Schuster, 2016.

Horton, Michael. *People and Place: A Covenant Ecclesiology*. Louisville: Westminster John Knox Press, 2008.

ABOUT THE DAVENANT INSTITUTE

The Davenant Institute supports the renewal of Christian wisdom for the contemporary church. It seeks to sponsor historical scholarship at the intersection of the church and academy, build networks of friendship and collaboration within the Reformed and evangelical world, and equip the saints with time-tested resources for faithful public witness.

We are a nonprofit organization supported by your tax-deductible gifts. Learn more about us, and donate, at www.davenantinstitute.org.